DRAMA

The Drama Classics series aims to offer the world's
greatest plays in affordable paperback editions for students,
actors and theatregoers. The hallmarks of the series are
accessible introductions, uncluttered texts and an overall
theatrical perspective.

Given that readers may be encountering a particular play
for the first time, the introduction seeks to fill in the
theatrical/historical background and to outline the chief
themes rather than concentrate on interpretational and
textual analysis. Similarly the play-texts themselves are free
of footnotes and other interpolations: instead there is an
end-glossary of 'difficult' words and phrases.

The texts of the English-language plays in the series
have been prepared taking full account of all existing
scholarship. The foreign-language plays have been newly
translated into a modern English that is both actable and
accurate: many of the translators regularly have their work
staged professionally.

Edited until his early death by Kenneth McLeish, the
Drama Classics series continues with his aim of providing
a first-class library of dramatic literature representing the
best of world theatre.

Associate editors:
Professor Trevor R. Griffiths
Dr. Colin Counsell
School of Arts and Humanities
University of North London

DRAMA CLASSICS *the first hundred*

*The publishers welcome
suggestions for further titles*

DRAMA CLASSICS

PHEDRA

by
Jean Racine

Translated and introduced by
Julie Rose

NICK HERN BOOKS
London

www.nickhernbooks.co.uk

A Drama Classic

This translation of *Phedra* first published in Great Britain
as a paperback original in 2001 by Nick Hern Books Limited,
14 Larden Road, London W3 7ST

Typeset by Country Setting, Kingsdown, Kent CT14 8ES
Printed by Bath Press

A CIP catalogue record for this book is available
from the British Library

ISBN 1 85459 094 4

Introduction

Jean Racine

Racine was born on 21 December 1639 into a family of
tax officials, local magistrates and artisans established for
over a hundred years in the small town of La Ferté-Milon,
north-east of Paris. His father Jean collected the tax on
salt; known as the *gabelle*, this tax had been imposed by
the kings of France in 1340. *Gabelleurs*, as collectors were
known, were increasingly unpopular in the sixteenth and
seventeenth centuries and would disappear with the
French Revolution.

Racine's mother, Jeanne Sconin, died a week after giving
birth to his sister Marie when Racine was only thirteen
months old. His father remarried but died in debt in 1643,
leaving Racine and Marie orphaned when the new wife
moved along. Racine was four, Marie, three. They were
separated and bundled off to each set of grandparents.

Racine went to his paternal grandparents, who were
devout Jansenists. Six years later, when Racine was ten,
his grandfather died, and he then became a ward of the
Jansenists as part of a package deal when his grandmother
signed on as a glorified *au pair* at the Jansenist abbey of
Port-Royal-des-Champs in the Chevreuse Valley near
Versailles.

The Jansenist connection is a formative one. La Ferté-Milon itself and Racine's extended family had close ties with 'Port-Royal'. Racine's grandmother had taken her profession of vows there in 1625. Her daughter Agnès would later become the abbess there; thirteen years older than Racine, Agnès remained a force to be reckoned with throughout his life. Racine's career as a privileged charity case began in one of the prestigious Jansenist junior schools, the *petites écoles*, run by Jansenist recluses known as *Solitaires* in the fields surrounding the abbey.

He could not have had a better education. The Jansenists – a no-frills sect within the Catholic Church opposed to the powerful Jesuits, who kept closing them down – offered the most progressive curriculum in France, beginning with French and including Ancient Greek on top of Latin. The Jesuits began with Latin, not French, and did not teach Greek at all. In the exact sciences, the Jansenists taught the very contemporary Descartes, whose idea of man-as-machine revolutionised French thought; they also went in for dissection. Fifty years later, Racine asked to be buried at the foot of his old science teacher, Dr. Hamon.

Others of Racine's teachers were some of the most illustrious in France, including Antoine Le Maître, once the star of French law. Le Maître taught Racine rhetoric, which meant composition, diction and declamation, three key elements in Racine's later theatre kit, as well as in his career, later still, as Louis XIV's preferred bedtime reader. (Racine's beautiful voice and reading style were renowned.) Le Maître also gave Racine his first books, setting up what was to become a very valuable collection.

Virtually alone of all the greats of this golden age of French theatre, Racine read the Greeks in the original; he later translated and annotated Aristotle, Plato, Sophocles and Euripides. In that shift from the baroque to the classical that took shape in the seventeenth century as the Quarrel between the Moderns and the Ancients, Racine would become the leading proponent in France of the – younger – Ancients, whose view of life was essentially tragic. The – older – Moderns were led by Pierre Corneille, thirty-three years Racine's senior and something of the grand old man of French theatre by the time Racine entered the scene. Baroque sensibility, with its zest for the fugitive and the mobile, often mingled with the more austere sensibility of neoclassicism, but the quarrel was fiercely fought and Racine, from the first, was an adept polemicist, promoting simplicity and authenticity as opposed to the Moderns' quivering refinement.

But before this, Racine was a young man about Paris, that great 'theatre of the world' where he went to study philosophy with the Jesuits in 1658. Paris was then still the seat of the Court as well as government, and the cultural life of the capital was vibrant. With charm and skill, Racine swiftly entered the *beau monde* and cultural elite. His circle of – lifelong – friends included the fabulist, La Fontaine, and the poet and essayist, Boileau, all of them 'Ancients' and a little wild. He and Boileau ended up together in the king's employ as twin royal historiographers. In the early days, they were regulars at salons such as that held by the brilliant *demi-mondaine,* Nina de Lenclos, famous for offering a heady 'sentimental education' to young men who appreciated a woman of wit.

For all this, Racine needed money and had none. There
were two main avenues available to him: the church and
literature, which had begun to offer serious money under
Louis XIV, Apollo of the arts, which he was busy
corporatising and sponsoring. The first option, pursued
through an uncle in the South of France, failed, so Racine
turned to writing.

He first turned to commemorative poetry with a poem in
praise of the Prime Minister, Mazarin, in 1659 after his
negotiation of peace with Spain. In 1660, an ode, *La
Nymphe de la Seine*, celebrated Louis XIV's marriage to
Maria Theresa of Spain, a hostage of the peace process.
The genre paid well if you could secure support, and
Racine's ode went down well with Chapelain, soon to
become the official channel for the bestowal of the king's
patronage. Another ode, *La Renommé aux muses*, written in
1661, was also appreciated as was his *Ode sur la convalescence
du roi* in 1663, celebrating Louis' return to health after a
bout of measles. Racine became Chapelain's protégé and
received a 'gratification' of 600 *livres* (pounds) in 1663-4,
his first literary takings.

From the outset, Racine had a nose for the patronage
game and conducted his career in the precarious and
shifting world of the Sun King's court with the same
virtuosity with which he turned out masterpiece after
masterpiece for the thirteen years of his theatrical glory.
As he wrote early in the piece to La Fontaine, 'one must
be tame with the tame, just as I've been a wolf with your
cohorts the wolves'.

The wolf could be fierce. Since the church was no go, he spurned the church. In 1663, he met Molière and was presented to the Court. He had already written two tragedies (which have disappeared without a trace) when Molière, by now the leading playwright in Paris after long hard years on the road, commissioned him to do a play in 1664. *La Thébiade*, produced in the June summer lull, was a strong debut. His second play, *Alexandre*, was performed by Molière's company at the end of 1665. But after only a few days, Racine whipped it away from Molière and gave it to the rival company at the Hôtel de Bourgogne. Although companies often performed competing versions of the same theme, Racine's material was not in the public domain, so his move was unusually ruthless. It is said that Molière never forgave him, particularly as Racine's defection to the Hôtel de Bourgogne, guaranteeing one play almost every winter for the next twelve years, made it the leading theatre company in Paris. But it is hard to imagine the two strongest force fields in all French theatre working together for long.

At this time, in 1665, the Jansenist theologian Nicole, a relative of Racine's, published a stinging attack on theatre in which he described playwrights as 'public poisoners'. Racine's counter-attack was so vicious it created fresh scandal. Nicole's view was one sanctioned not only by Pascal, the leading light of Jansenism whom Racine so admired; it was still sanctioned by the orthodox Catholic Church, with which, it should be remembered, Louis XIV was often in conflict (until his later years when he, and the Court with him, settled into a grim piety). With

publication of part of this tract in 1666, Racine's rupture
with Port-Royal was complete. It is worth noting, though,
that this very public break occurred just after an official
crackdown on Port-Royal in 1664.

In November 1667, *Andromaque*, created for a court audience,
was a huge hit. It starred Thérèse Du Parc, who had
defected to Racine's company with her husband after two
years with Molière. In 1667, she was blonde and beautiful
and, at thirty-five, nearly ten years older than Racine. It
was thought she was the love of his life; they were even
rumoured to have secretly married and to have had a
daughter who died at the age of eight. La Du Parc herself
suddenly died in 1668. (Racine was very nearly arrested
for her murder in 1680 as an offshoot of the scandal of
the century known as 'The Poison Affair', but the order
for his arrest was quashed – possibly by the king himself.)

1668 was also the year Racine wrote his only comedy, *Les
Plaideurs*, a send-up of parliament and the legal profession
featuring that most French creature, the dog. Though a
bit of a flop at the time, it remains one of the most
performed of Racine's plays.

With such successes under his belt, and having
demonstrated a virtuoso versatility, Racine seems to have
decided to take on Corneille, a towering figure since his
debut in 1629, with masterworks such as *Le Cid* and
L'Illusion comique. Racine produced a rival *Britannicus* at the
end of 1669 and a rival *Bérénice* in 1670, performed
initially before the Court and then at the Hôtel de
Bourgogne. Racine's versions eclipsed Corneille's and
contributed to Corneille's decline.

Entering the contemporary craze for things Turkish, Racine created *Bajazet* early in 1672. It was published almost immediately and was followed by the re-editing of *Alexandre*. Racine's pre-eminence was now official. In 1673 he was admitted to the Académie française. His inaugural speech, delivered on 12 January, fell a little flat but the next day a new play *Mithridate* opened and the revised *Andromaque* was published.

In August 1674, *Iphigénie* was performed at Versailles as part of royal festivities (Louis XIV had commissioned the building of Versailles as a showpiece of French genius in arts and governance in 1674). In October, Racine became Trésorier de France, stationed at Moulins, a mere title. In 1676, an edition of his collective works was brought out, an extraordinary event for a living playwright, unprecedented for one only thirty-seven years old.

On 1 January 1677, he created *Phèdre et Hippolyte* (published in March that year and, as *Phèdre*, in the collected works of 1689). Racine created the role of Phedra for La Champmeslé, the dazzling actress who replaced La Du Parc on stage and in Racine's life (her husband played Theseus and seems not to have minded the liaison). 'Ugly close up, adorable on stage', in the words of Madame de Sévigné whose son was also involved with her, La Champmeslé was the finest actress of her day. For Racine, she had already played Bérénice and Iphigénie.

Though generally considered since as his greatest masterpiece, *Phèdre's* initial reception was fraught with political tensions peculiar to the times. The Moderns represented by Corneille got wind of what Racine was writing; one of their party, Pradon, immediately tossed off his own version simultaneously. Racine's enemies went to great lengths to trash the play, buying up most of the seats to ensure a near-empty auditorium or hissing and boo-ing with gusto. But the king finally gave Racine the nod and Pradon's audience dropped off, his play sinking without a trace.

Racine never wrote for the theatre-going public again. His dramatic retreat – on such a high note – is sometimes attributed to bitterness. Others have seen it as a step higher up the ladder of his endless social climb. Two things are worth noting. One is that, only months after *Phèdre,* Racine married Catherine de Romanet, a distant relative who brought to the marriage an estate on a par with Racine's own, by now considerable. It was her boast that she had never been to the theatre in her life and had no interest in going. The second is that, the same year, Racine was named, with Boileau, historiographer to the king. In the peculiar context of the Sun-King's universe, this was an honour without equal, one that also brought in an exceptional gratification of 6000 *livres.*

Whether under his pious wife's influence or because the Court itself was becoming increasingly austere under the influence of the king's last favourite, Madame de Maintenon, Racine renewed his ties with Port-Royal in 1679 and regularly interceded with the king on the Jansenists' behalf even when it was reckless to do so. He was a devoted family man, father of five daughters and two sons, who followed his childrens' lives closely, affectionately and fussily, as letters to his eldest son,

Jean-Baptiste, show. (Jean-Baptiste would later burn many of his father's papers, upon Racine's request, and we'll never know what it was he was wanting to hide.)

Racine's writing after *Phèdre* was largely confined to his work as a hack historian, with a potted history of the king's campaigns based on observations in the field that had courtiers guffawing as they pictured Racine trotting along behind the king in the mud of the battlefield, madly scribbling notes which the gouty Boileau, safely ensconced at home, would then transcribe. He did write one good history, though, a biting account of the Jansenists. But this was a secret project and when word of it leaked, it cost him his standing with the king (who was to have Port-Royal burned down, finally, in 1713 as his own parting shot). Some thought Racine never recovered from the blow.

No one could not regret Racine's renunciation after *Phèdre*. There would be just two 'religious' plays after this, commissioned by Madame de Maintenon for the exclusive girls' school she founded: *Esther* in 1689, *Athalie* in 1691. That was it. From 1664 to 1677, from *La Thébiade* to *Phèdre*, via *Bérénice* and *Iphigénie*, there had been thirteen years of exploration of the human soul, thirteen years of masterpieces and success. Yet this seems to have been of no account once Racine got the call from the Sun King, he who considered himself annointed by God to rule and to embody the France of the previous twelve hundred years. We have to imagine a world in which the gift of the Sun King's presence, the inestimable honour of recording his every move, were of greater value than anything else Racine had achieved.

Racine described this honour – sincerely – in his address
on 2 January 1685 to the Academy as one where he got:
'To study [the king] in his most minor daily activities, no
less great, no less heroic, no less admirable, full of equity,
full of humanity, always calm, always in control, without
shifts of humour, without weakness, always the wisest and
most perfect of men.' When relations with Madame de
Maintenon soured in 1698 – possibly because of Racine's
overzealous defence of the Jansenists – he was
inconsolable. According to Saint-Simon, he 'felt such
chagrin that he fell ill and only lived another two years'.

As has been said by others, without the king, Molière
would have continued to shine for century after century;
without the king, Racine would not have abandoned
theatre so early and become ossified in hagiography – or
minor works, such as an opera with Boileau in 1683 and
another in 1685, *Idylle sur la paix* (*Idyl on Peace*), set to music
by Lully as a royal party piece. On the other hand, without
the king's patronage, he might not have written at all.

Disenchanted or not, Racine died of cancer at sixty in
1699, ennobled, safely wealthy and with three editions of
collected works to his name.

The Theatre in Racine's Day

In 1660, when Racine first hit town, there were six theatre
troupes in Paris. The Hôtel de Bourgogne near the Palais
Royal was the most prestigious, specialising in tragedy and
enjoying the royal seal of approval, '*Troupe du Roy*'. The
royal players were known as '*Grands Comédiens*'.

The Hôtel also hosted the Italian commedia dell'arte from 1653 until 1658 when they moved in with Molière; and it hosted the Spanish Players who came from Spain with Maria-Theresa in 1663 – until they returned in 1672. Not far away, the Théâtre du Marais had been going since the beginning of the century, coming into its own from the mid-1630s with Pierre Corneille. By the late 1650s it had fallen on hard times, revived by '*pièces à machines*' such as Corneille's *La Toison d'or* (*The Golden Fleece*) in 1661, typically featuring mechanical set changes and effects.

The Petit-Bourbon under the colonnade of the Louvre housed the '*Troupe de Monsieur*', 'Monsieur' being Louis XIV's brother, which was directed by Molière from 1658 when he settled in Paris. The shortlived '*Comédiens de Mademoiselle*' at the Faubourg St.-Germain vanished in 1662.

By 1673, the year Molière died and Racine reigned as king of tragedy at the Hôtel de Bourgogne with eight plays under his belt, the theatre scene consolidated, like every other area of cultural life under the Sun King. The Marais company fused with Molière's and, in July 1673, the '*Troupe du Guénégaud*' kicked off with a revival of Molière's *Tartuffe*, originally banned in 1664.

This means there were now only two decent theatres in Paris: the Hôtel de Bourgogne, directed by Racine, and the Hôtel de Guénégaud, directed by La Grange, the actor who took over from Molière. The theatre scene became even more savage than it is today, when issues of 'intellectual property' have become paramount. The rivalry could be stimulating; it only intensified as diversity and funding dwindled, and it was common for playwrights, even of the calibre of Corneille, to steal the ideas or theme of a rival's play as it was being written – spies were everywhere – in order to pip them at the post.

Once rival plays opened, no tactic was too base in the scramble to damage the enemy's credibility or audience share. Racine's pre-eminence can be measured by the ferocity of such campaigns against him (conspirators, representing opposed political camps, were known as 'the cabal'). The more celebrated he became, the dirtier the opposition. This culminated in the attack on *Phèdre*. Far from sitting back and enjoying the usual spur to box-office, as he had done with *Iphigénie* and *Bérénice*, Racine seems to have tried to have Pradon's rival version shut down.

Pradon's rent-a-crowd hissed and boo-ed *Phèdre* and bought up dummy seats; they publicly decried Racine's 'immorality' – in Pradon's coy version, Phedra is Theseus' fiancée, not his wife, and there is no suicide (a mortal sin then as now in the view of the Catholic Church). A satirical sonnet was bandied about to the effect that Racine's Phedra spoke gibberish.

Racine was furious, which gives some idea how important the play was to him. He heaped verbal abuse on Pradon's protector, the duc de Nevers, though it was not Nevers but a woman, the playwright Deshouilles, who had written the sonnet . . . Top level diplomatic intervention saw Racine apologising to Nevers and all of Paris laughing into its cups until the shenanigans subsided and Racine's broadest-ever audience acknowledged his play as a supreme masterpiece.

Racine was no stranger to dirty tactics himself as his treatment of Molière shows. It also shows how early in the piece he knew he need not play second fiddle, which he was forced to do by the rules of theatre programming: plays were produced as an after-dinner double, with the main feature a 'serious' play, followed by a comedy or farce – an arrangement that let theatregoers leave on a high note before flitting off to supper.

Racine also managed to lure performers away from other companies. This he did with both his star actresses, the Marquise Du Parc and her successor, La Champmeslé, who both came in the expectation of better roles and better pay. The monetary value of star players could reach dizzying heights. Two years after *Phèdre*, for instance, the Champmeslé couple was bought up by the Hôtel de Guénégaud for sums not unlike those offered to football players today. La Champmeslé was the first 'star' in the modern sense, thanks to Racine.

Theatre was the air Racine breathed; he was one of the troupe, tirelessly rehearsing his actors, reworking the script, which went through several drafts after actors, friends and luminaries had had their say. For *Phèdre*, treading on eggshells as he perhaps felt himself by then to be, he even had the script vetted by two celebrated Jesuit priests: it was not heretical, not Jansenist or blasphemous. Racine could face the music.

And the music on opening night must have been something to face. Seventeenth-century audiences were noisy and distracted at the best of times, when they wandered around in the well of the Hôtel de Bourgogne, a long narrow room like a tennis court, eating and drinking and shouting comments. This was the worst, with Pradon's team hurling abuse and perhaps more concrete missiles under the flaming candelabra as Racine's actors tried to make themselves heard. It would have strained Racine's signature naturalistic style. Perhaps he looked forward to the stints in the royal apartments at the Louvre or Versailles or in the summer palaces of Fontainebleau and Sceaux. At Court, though, his work would have had to compete with the big *son et lumière* productions that Louis XIV was famous for.

What Happens Before the Play Begins

As in all great literature, a lot happens in *Phèdre* before the play begins. The story goes back to the origins of Greek mythology, not so very long ago in the timeframe of the play, when the Sky and the Earth mated and gave birth to the Titans, Time and the Sun. Phedra's prestige comes from her royal lineage, for she is directly descended from the Sun through her mother, Pasiphae, daughter of the Sun; on her father's side, she is directly descended from Jupiter, King of the Gods, who produced her father Minos, King of Crete, now judge of the dead in Hades.

Minos and Pasiphae married and had two daughters, Ariadne and Phedra. But Pasiphae also gave birth to a monster, the Minotaur, half-man, half-bull. Racine's audience was perfectly familiar with the tale of the Minotaur, and it would have been for them a shimmering image of doomed lust, or the doom of lust. Minos had become too attached to a handsome bull he was meant to sacrifice to Neptune, whose gift to him it was. Neptune took his revenge by making Pasiphae fall madly in love with the bull, giving birth to the Minotaur after a typically weird bit of interspecies adultery.

So in Racine's poetics, the story of the Minotaur is a key element in the theme of sinful attachment. It's also where Theseus comes in and the more recent history begins, for the Minotaur is slain by the young Theseus, Greece's greatest hero. This comes about because of another injustice and another curse. Theseus' father, Aegeus, King of Athens, had sent Minos' son on a dangerous hunt for a wild bull when the young man was visiting Athens from his native Crete. The bull killed him, proving what a bad host Aegeus was. Minos invaded Athens and threatened to destroy the city unless, every nine years, the Athenians sent him seven young male and seven young female virgins, to be devoured by the Minotaur whom Minos had not slain but kept in a famous labyrinth designed by the architect Daedalus. No one could find their way out of the labyrinth, so the fourteen virgins went inevitably to their deaths.

Young and keen, Theseus got himself included in the cortege one year, secretly planning to kill the Minotaur with his bare hands – which he promptly did. He was aided in his triumph by Ariadne, who had fallen in love with him and given him a ball of string to help him retrace his steps out of the labyrinth. In return, Theseus carted Ariadne off and dumped her on the island of Naxos. (There are kinder versions of the story, but Racine follows this one in which Theseus seduces and abandons alluring women until he meets his match in Phedra, who is able to 'tame' him.)

Another part of the story that tells us something about Theseus is that he forgot to hoist the white flag that would tell Aegeus he was returning triumphant to Athens (the ship of virgins sailed under a black flag). His father spotted the black flag coming and threw himself in despair into the sea, forever after known the Aegean.

Guilty passion, monsters, labyrinths, bad kings, thoughtless heroes, the spiteful wilfulness of the Gods: it's all there, as resonating décor, before the story of Phedra herself properly begins. Her story is that she alone, hero/monster-tamer, won by now ageing Theseus' heart for good and so was 'abducted into marriage' by him. On the very day of her wedding in Athens, she met Theseus' son, Hippolytus, a ravishing young athlete dedicated to the cult of chastity, and fell hopelessly in love with him. In the violent – and noble – struggle against her feelings that the play will violently resolve, Phedra has done all she can do to distance herself from Hippolytus; mistreating him, exiling him to Troezen, the town in southern Greece where Theseus spent his childhood (with his mother), banning his name. Time has passed. She has had two sons by her lawful husband, she has lived the life of a virtuous wife and mother, an arid but irreproachable life.

But Theseus has gone off again on one of his adventures with his randy pal Pirithous, after bringing his wife to Troezen and consigning her to Hippolytus' care. Wrapped in the oblivion of pointless heroism, he has undone all her work. The renewed effort of trying to overcome her secret passion has made her sick to the point of advanced anorexia. When we see her, she is dying – a lonely and heroic death, for still no one knows what ails her.

What Happens in the Play

The storyline of *Phèdre* is a beautifully simple love chain: Theseus loves his wife Phedra, who loves his son Hippolytus, who loves his enemy Aricia, who loves Hippolytus back but can't legitimately have him. No one is happy; no love has divine blessing; even love's young dream is cursed.

The tale the play tells begins when Theseus has been gone six months. Hippolytus is fretting for him and decides to embark on another search. Phedra is about to take her secret to the grave when her maid Oenon, frantic to save the woman for whom she has given up everything, gets the truth out of her. The news then arrives that Theseus is dead. Oenon persuades Phedra that his death legitimizes her love for Hippolytus and that she needs him on side for political reasons, in any case, since there is an immediate power struggle out there in the background of real events between herself, her young son and Hippolytus.

Hippolytus meanwhile has approached Aricia, the young woman Racine has invented as the surviving sister of the Pallas brothers killed by Theseus during their grab for power. Aricia is taboo as a political enemy, but Hippolytus is in love with her anyhow and seeks to restore her freedom the moment Theseus is declared dead. In an outburst that preludes Phedra's, he confesses his love.

They are interrupted by Phedra, hoping to console Hippolytus for his father's death. But she, too, is overcome and reveals all. His horror at her declaration of love for him is such that, with escalating violence, Phedra invites him to stab her through the heart with his sword; grabs it to do the deed herself but is saved by Oenon. News immediately arrives that Athens has voted her young son king and that she herself now rules Athens until he comes of age.

Despite Oenon's scorn, Phedra swings round to hope, imagining that she alone of all women will be able to 'tame' Hippolytus and cause him to feel love. She implores Venus, the goddess who has cursed her – and unbeknown to her, Hippolytus as well – to 'make him love . . . ' It is at this moment, exactly half-way through the play when tragic irony has hit a peak, that the news explodes that Theseus is alive and well and on his way. His return is the beginning of the end sealing Phedra's doom, as she tells Oenon: 'This morning I was dying; I would have been mourned. / I took your advice and die disgraced.'

Oenon persuades Phedra that Hippolytus will expose her so that she must get in first and accuse him of trying to rape her, using the evidence of the sword he left behind. Phedra goes along with the plan, mostly letting Oenon do the dirty work of bearing false witness. Theseus, the bad father, no doubt jealous of his son, reacts more violently than anticipated, calling on Neptune to punish his son in full knowledge that this means Hippolytus' death. Hippolytus begs for mercy, confesses his love for Aricia as his only sin, but Theseus banishes him with a vicious curse. Phedra hears the curse and is panicked into telling the truth, but before she can speak Theseus tells her that Hippolytus claims to love Aricia. For Theseus it is a ploy; for Phedra, it is the sword through the heart that turns love to jealousy and hate. She decides to let Hippolytus die.

And die he does – a horrible death, recounted in gory detail by Theramenes. Phedra kills herself by taking a poison Medea brought with her from Crete, but not before restoring Hippolytus' good name. In one of the legitimisation processes with which Racine anoints his finales, Theseus adopts Aricia as his daughter.

The Structure of the Play

Phèdre is considered Racine's best-built play. We can see how tightly it is put togther if we look at the pivotal event of Theseus' rumoured return. 'The King we thought was dead is on his way' is line 827 in a play of 1654 lines. With breathtaking simplicity, Racine slices the play precisely in half along an axis that reverses the whole situation. It rings like a death sentence for Phedra at the very moment she had decided to live. And it announces the condition for the descent into the maelstrom with the monstrous massacre of Hippolytus – in name and in body – that will ensue, along with the suicides of Oenon and Phedra and the beginnings of the demise of Theseus as king.

On either side of this pivotal axis lies symmetry, orchestrated into a kind of symphony of themes and arias. Phedra, Theseus' second wife, loves Hippolytus, the son of his first marriage to the Amazon, Antiope. When she believes herself to be dying, she confesses her love twice, once to Oenon, once to Hippolytus himself. When she believes Theseus to be dead, she begins to hope for union with Hippolytus. When Theseus suddenly returns, her love once again becomes a crime. As a cover, two false

accusations of attempted rape are then made against
Hippolytus, one actively made by Oenon, one a lie of
omission committed by Phedra (though she could also be
said to have dropped a pretty heavy hint when Theseus
first reappears).

Hippolytus has broken a (less compelling) taboo by falling
in love with Aricia, who is held hostage by Theseus
and prohibited from marrying. He admits his love to
Theramenes in the opening scene; he then admits his love
to Aricia herself, propelled headlong as Phedra will shortly
be by the sight of the object of his love. After Theseus'
return, he also admits his love to Theseus, though Theseus
misreads this as a ploy and won't believe him. Theseus
scornfully relays the story to Phedra who does believe it
and this seals her lips and so seals Hippolytus' doom.

Before Theseus' return, Phedra suffers guilty love in
silence, keen to die; then she suffers from breaking that
silence; afterwards, she suffers a new emotion, jealousy,
then commits in silence the monstrous 'blackening of
innocence'. Hippolytus suffers guilty love in silence, is
released by breaking that silence but then doomed by
keeping the truth about Phedra silent from Theseus. He
will not 'blacken' guilt, speak the unspeakable, even to
save his life. Phedra will only tell the truth at the cost of
her life when it is too late to save Hippolytus.

Operatic echoes are set off between Hippolytus'
stammering declaration of love to Aricia and Phedra's to
him. Love's young dream, erupting in a surge of emotion
that bursts through the thin veneer of civilised discourse,
feebly parallels Phedra's hallucinatory paroxysm, when she

recites to Hippolytus the calamity of falling in love with him at first sight. Critics (mostly gay) have attacked Hippolytus as 'feminine', the modern critic Roland Barthes going so far as to suggest Racine gave Hippolytus Aricia simply to make more of a man of him. It is true Hippolytus suffers from impotence – that of a man of action who hasn't yet been called on to act. But the Hippolytus that Phedra depicts is hot – though it's true we traditionally associate being an object of lust with femininity and see lust as masculine. Racine is not so limited; both Hypolytus' fiercely virginal virility and Phedra's (perfectly feminine) virility in savouring it are overwhelmingly convincing in justly celebrated monologues that sizzle on the page.

The play has been called a tragedy of language, meaning that what happens is the result of acts of speech – or their omission. Declaration of love, accusation, curse and banishment: everything hinges on these four linguistic acts. What is said is as effective as any deed, altering the course of events, dealing death (banishment leads to death twice: Oenon's before Hippolytus'). Speech derails. When Phedra declares her love to Hippolytus, he is stunned, immobilised (with horror, certainly, and perhaps something else); it is she who unsheathes his sword to stab herself and thereby achieve symbolic penetration.

The sword is loaded with meaning. It works as an obvious phallic symbol and as a sign of Phedra's consciousness of this as she tries to manipulate it; it is equally a symbol of Hippolytus' purity as the bearer of a paternal legacy not yet initiated into the manly endeavours his father (and his Amazon mother) would normally hope to bequeath him.

That sword is aching to be used. And it is used – against Hippolytus, as false evidence, symbolically decimating him. Theseus: 'The brute used force./I recognised his sword, the same sword/ I gave him for a nobler purpose.'

The sword becomes one of many signs misread by Theseus as he staggers through his homecoming, punch-drunk and steering without a compass. The clearest signs are culpably misread: Hippolytus' face, 'his noble bearing', the way he seems 'to glow with virtue', not to mention his life, as Aricia points out in her feisty exchange with Theseus after Hippolytus has fled.

But then, Theseus is the morally blind hero, who symbolically kills his own father by forgetting to stick to the agreed signal. He fatally misreads his wife and has done so always.

Nor do we feel no sympathy with Theseus, lousy father and husband that he is. For if the gods hate humanity, Racine, one feels, does not. One of the very moving features of the play is the way Theseus stirs our compassion even as he demonstrates his stupidity. For he is that useless thing, the man of action, completely out of his depth in the swirling sea of emotion that washes round him and drowns him. He loses everything. One of the great ringing lines of the play belongs to him and we can't help but feel its charge: 'I hate the Gods – down to the very gifts they've lavished upon me.'

Place and People in the Play

There are places in Racine that go back to the beginnings of time, to some original pinnacle of rock and sky. The place where *Phèdre* takes place seems frozen in some archaic blight of heat, where sun and dust can only be escaped by sea (this option being available only to plebs and heroes); or in the forest, hidden from view (Phedra admiring Hippolytus as he careens round the race track in his chariot; Hippolytus and Aricia projected as happy ideal lovers in Phedra's jealous imagination); or inside the palace, that dark pit of destructive passions where the only action that matters will be played out.

You never see the outside world in *Phèdre*, you only hear of it from the messengers that flit in and out, picking up vital information with the speed of jets. The outside world is an abstract entity where Theseus slays monsters or is trapped in Hell and the mob of Athens roars and elects rulers.

There is one vital exception to this rule and it concerns the all-important light of day: the sun. One of the powerful metaphors of Phedra's torment is her need to let in the light and her desire to shut it out and hide in darkness. The light flags Phedra's nobility, her magnifence and of course it signals truth, rightness, purity – defiled and finally restored. In that incandescent dying speech, where Phedra typically burns and freezes to death, she describes dying as a blinding force whereby 'Death steals the light from my eyes / And returns it to the day I darkened / All its shining purity restored'. What an image to go out on!

There's a tremendous feeling of heat in *Phèdre*, of the sun boring down, bearing implacable destiny with it, of searing lust burning Phedra's body to cinders no matter what she tries to do. A hot wind blows through the play, scorching, violent and elemental. All the heat and lust, chills and fevers, define that elemental world of the Greek Gods that Racine depicts as both the intimate calamity of the story and the big picture of forces completely beyond human control.

What is remarkable is the easy interplay between these levels: elements of mythology – especially the losing battle between rival goddesses Venus and Diana – and the physical, psychological forces at work, presented both metaphorically and with a blood-and-guts realism that takes your breath away. This blend reminds us of 17th century architecture: outside, geometric rigour; inside, chaos. When Phedra describes the lust torturing her, no wall of abstraction can protect us from the heat of her description. Everywhere you look there's a physicality so basic as to be beyond crude, splintering the porcelain fineness of the language, shattering control of speech. This extremism, sustained on all levels, makes the play uniquely powerful.

It is often said that Phedra completely dominates the play. Racine's array of wonderful women is unique in theatre: Hermione, Andromaque, Bérénice, Iphigénie, Roxane, Phedra and Athalie.

But look how rich and perfect even the 'lesser' characters are. Oenon, for instance, sketched in effortlessly as a complete personality: patrician – her mistress is, after all, semi-divine – yet with a perfect touch of the fish-wife, vulgar, scheming and yet very moving at the same time. Her lucidity about her behaviour parallels Phedra's own and her suicide after Phedra banishes her is a powerfully cruel self-judgement preluding Phedra's. The characterisation is so complete, we feel a great deal more sympathy with her than Phedra does when she heaps blame on the 'vile Oenon' in her dying speech, for Oenon's story is also one of great love and loss.

The pair formed by Phedra and her maid is paralleled, almost parodied, by Aricia and her maid Ismen. The wonderful girlie scene they have before Hippolytus appears is the play's only light relief, and it is done as deftly as everything else. Aricia has had a hard time over the years. Sarah Bernhardt, who had a brief stint as Aricia in 1873, before moving on to Phedra, called her an ambitious little bourgeois upstart. And so she is, endearingly so: 'No easy victory for me. I'm far prouder.' This is a girl thing, from a warrior princess, yet her virginal virility matches Hippolytus' own, and for all her girlish dreams of power, we've just heard the note of genuine lust in her appraisal of him. Her later prudish pitch for marriage smacks of a vulnerability that sits comfortably with her strength in challenging Theseus.

These master-servant relationships are always quietly at work in Racine. The couple formed by Hippolytus and his tutor Theramenes has a lot to say about the (complex) conflict between father and son in the play. Theramenes is the good father: kind, observant, rightly appreciative. He knows Hippolytus' secret, he's watched him; he gently encourages his love. Note the ironic parallels with Phedra and Oenon: for this love is 'natural', the taboo against Aricia is an unjust taboo imposed by Theseus – the once celebrated democrat now perverted into a tyrant. The contrast between Theramenes and Theseus is highlighted from the very beginning, for Theseus is, above all, absent.

The contrast between father and son is also presented in the opening scene in Hippolytus' narrative of Theseus' tarnished record, preparing us for the breathtaking hallucination Phedra slips into when she sees Hippolytus and remembers seeing him for the first time, overlaying this vision with a vision of Theseus as he was. Hippolytus is Theseus as he was, only better: 'loyal, lofty and a bit fierce'. Theseus was then the 'cream of Greece's heroes' but quickly became 'a fickle philanderer with a roving eye' – a boor; Hippolytus is the real thing. Some buried consciousness of this pushes Theseus into what amounts to regicide. Regicide/parricide (Aegeus), parricide (his son): Theseus ends up with a lot of (his own) blood on his hands.

Has there ever been so much talk of blood? Racine covers the blood spectrum, ultimately flinging at us the sacrificial body of Hippolytus, bloody mangle, blood-matted hair strewn over the rocks; hands are dipped in innocent blood; blood burns through the body in lust, freezes in horror, terror and death. Though it is often a metaphor, it is also the real stuff that circulates in the body. With Phedra's body and the things that happen to it, you have the fastest blood in theatre – and a dazzling emotional range to which she brings an almost scientific lucidity.

The Playing of *Phedra* in France and England

Between 1680, when the Comédie Française, France's National Theatre, was formed, and 1997, roughly 1460 performances of *Phédre* have been given in its theatre at the Palais-Royal in Paris alone. It is impossible to know how many times the play has been staged around the world but what is certain is that it continues to be staged and to challenge and move modern audiences relentlessly.

Two productions in 1998, one in Paris, one in London, show how vital the play remains, with very different interpretations of the text and of the role of Phedra in particular pointing to how many questions the play still asks us and the endless ways in which these can be framed. For three centuries audiences have been debating the meaning of the play and they still do, as hotly – a masterpiece is inexhaustible.

Is Racine a fatalist, flying in the face of the Catholic doctrine of free will? Is there 'no escape from destiny'? Can Phedra possibly act differently from the way she does? Is there sin, can there be blame? Does remorse make any sense? Proust thought the play was Jansenist, showcasing the pain and terror of human beings buffeted by forces beyond their control. A century before him, Chateaubriand thought it an exemplary Christian tale of a fallen woman. The issue remains critical and, in the end, comes down to how big a monster, if at all, Phedra is seen to be, for Phedra is the fulcrum on which everyone else pivots. In other words, how do we feel about Phedra?

The Phedra offered by Luc Bondy's Paris production at the Odéon theatre (September-October 1998) was a convincingly contemporary monster. Played by the young Valérie Dréville, she quietly unravelled, swinging between regality and the psychotic state into which she sinks. This Phedra is inhabited by a cancerous desire for possession that makes her a monster and kills her.

That production was interesting also because of the playing down of the alexandrine, the modern cadences given to Racine's poetry often working against the direction of the narration and playing for madness in an hallucinogenic landscape of sand.

Narrative-driven and more superficially contemporary, Jonathan Kent's production for the Almeida in London (at the same time in 1998) showed a ravaged Diana Rigg, so much older than Hippolytus she could easily have been his mother, playing for pathos. Most notable modern Phedras have been older women, from French actresses Maria Casarès (1958) and Marie Bell (1962) to British actress Glenda Jackson (at the Old Vic in 1984).

The question of Phedra's age will apparently always be an issue. Does it matter? Sarah Bernhardt (1844-1923), the most famous Phedra of all time, would have said no. To prove it, she played Phedra from the age of twenty-nine until she was well into her sixties. Then again, Bernhardt was French and the French have never had that Anglo-Saxon problem with age (in women). More to the point, at any age, Bernhardt was sexy.

And that is far more important than the issue of Phedra's age: Phedra has sexual authority. She is not just queenly, she shimmers with sexual allure – even as the enfeebled anorexic we see stumbling under the weight of her veils, those trappings of the queenly state. That is how she got to tame Theseus and 'fixed his wandering eye on her'. Hippolytus says so in the opening scene. He clearly can't be oblivious to her power. And her power must be startling, for Helen of Troy is one of the many acts Phedra has to follow.

One minute of Bernhardt's Phedra can be heard on tape (available from Editions des femmes, Paris). Speeded-up and shrill, that minute still conveys something of the silvery clarity of Bernhardt's voice and the robustness of her performance. In fact her performance was so robust, she regularly passed out and sometimes vomited blood – even though she was most often only doing the monologues for she rarely performed the whole play. The monologues were enough. Audiences in France, England and America went wild. At the Gaiety Theatre in London on the 1879 tour, they sobbed uncontrollably as Bernahrdt gave them, in her words, 'my blood . . . my life . . . my soul'. That, in a nutshell, is the challenge of the role.

For Further Reading

One of the sharpest critical essays on Racine's theatre is
Roland Barthes, *On Racine* (1960 for the French, *Sur
Racine;* 1964 for the English translation) and there are
several editions of both the French and the English
around.

There are many biographies. One of the best is Alain
Viala, *Racine, la stratégie du caméléon* (Seghers: Paris, 1990).
Viala's tone is strangely snide but he offers a wealth of
detail and I've borrowed heavily from his book for the
present introduction. Viala acknowledges his own debt to
R. Picard, *La Carrière de Jean Racine* (reissued by Gallimard:
Paris, 1998). Novelist François Mauriac's bleak and
imaginary life of Racine makes an interesting contrast.

For more solid detail, see the Port-Royal exhibition
catalogue, *Phèdre, Racine, le Choix de l'absolu* (Editions de la
Réunion des Musées nationaux: Paris, 1999).

Dip into any great French writer from Voltaire, Diderot,
Chateaubriand and Proust to Gide and Duras, and you
will find something on Racine and *Phèdre*. For a
fascinating historical perspective see Stendhal, *Racine et
Shakespeare: Etudes sur le Romantisme*.

There are plenty of useful English-language works as well,
one of the best being David Maskell, *Racine: A Theatrical
Reading* (Oxford University Press, 1991). See also Ronald

W. Tobin, *Jean Racine Revisited* (Twayne's World Authors Series: New York, 1999) and Michael Hawcroft, *Word as Action: Racine, Rhetoric and Theatrical Language* (Oxford Modern Languages and Literature Monographs, 1992).
All decent collected works of Racine and scholarly editions of *Phèdre* provide useful notes.

Racine: Key Dates

1639 Born on 21 December in La Ferté-Milon, only son of Jean Racine and Jeanne Sconin.

January 1641 A sister, Marie, is born; Jeanne dies a week later from childbirth complications.

September 1642 Racine's father dies three months after remarrying.

1643-1649 Racine lives with his paternal grandparents.

1649 Racine's grandfather dies; his grandmother joins the Jansenist convent of Port-Royal-des-Champs. Racine is taken on as a non-paying boarder at one of the exclusive *Petites Ecoles* nearby.

1653-1655 Advanced classes at Beauvais College.

1655-1658 Back at Port-Royal for Rhétorique Supérieure.

1658-1659 Moves to Paris to study Philosophy at the Harcourt, lodging with his cousin, an intendant, in the duc de Luynes' private hotel.

1659 Launches his literary career with commemorative poetry.

Amasie, his first play, is offered to Molière, rejected and lost; his first published poem, 'Ode de la Nymphe de la Seine à la Reine', is a success.

1661-1662   Stays with an uncle, a canon in Uzès, in a bid to join the priesthood but the plan fails.

1663   Opts for the literary life in Paris. His 'Ode sur la convalescence du roi' attracts Chapelain, busy orchestrating France's new cultural policy with the Minister, Colbert. 'La Renommée aux Muses' celebrates Louis XIV's marriage to Maria Theresa of Spain. He offers Molière a second play, *Ovide*, also rejected and lost.

June 1664   *La Thébaïde ou les frères ennemis* debuts with Molière's theatre. Racine earns 348 francs in box office and is awarded his first royal gratification of 600 *livres* – soon raised to 800, 1200, then 1500 by 1670.

December 1665   *Alexandre le Grand* opens at Molière's theatre. Ten days later, Racine gives it to the rival Hôtel de Bourgogne, despite Molière's exclusive rights. Racine is paid twice for the same play in a well-planned coup. Like all Racine's plays, the text is published promptly – in January 1666.

1666   Racine's *Lettre à l'auteur des Hérésies imaginaires*, refuting the accusation by Jansenist, Nicole, that playwrights are 'public poisoners', is published 'anonymously'. Racine's break with 'Port-Royal' is violent.

November 1667   *Andromaque*, based on Euripides and performed first at Court then at the Hôtel de Bourgogne with Racine's lover Thérèse Du Parc in the title role, is a triumph.

1668   Thérèse Du Parc dies. Racine appears 'half-dead' with grief at her funeral but her mother will later accuse him of poisoning her daughter.

December 1668   *Les Plaideurs*, Racine's only comedy, is a flop.

December 1669   *Britannicus* has to compete with a spectacular public execution; it is forced to close after only seven shows, making it Racine's greatest failure. His Preface redefines tragedy as a 'pared down' form and speaks of 'characters' rather than 'actors'.

December 1670   *Bérénice* competes with Corneille's rival *Tite et Bérénice*. Starring La Champmeslé, Racine's play moves the audience to tears. His Preface says theatre should simply aim 'to please and to move'.

January 1672   *Bajazet*, a fashionably 'Turkish' Harem tragedy, is a hit.

December 1672   *Mithridate* reworks old themes for the Court during Christmas festivities.

12 January 1673   Racine is inducted into the Académie Française at age 33, the youngest academician in its thirty-six year history.

Autumn/Winter 1673-4   *Iphigénie* marks a magnificent return to the Greek myths, produced first at Court then at the Hôtel de Bourgogne to great acclaim. The Preface attacks the 'Moderns' via Euripides.

1674   Racine buys a post as 'Conseiller trésorier de France et général des finances en la généralité de Moulins' i.e. he becomes a tax collector in a small provincial town – in name only, unlike his father before him.

January 1676   Racine brings out his first *Oeuvres complètes*, making himself a 'classic' at only 36.

January-March 1677   *Phèdre et Hippolyte* plays at the
Hôtel de Bourgogne while a rival play by Pradon plays
at the Hôtel de Guénégaud. It then rivets the Court at
Sceaux and Fontainebleau during the summer carnival
and is hailed as a masterpiece. The Preface claims
theatre's first duty is to instruct.

Racine turns his back on 'profane theatre' and never
writes another play for public consumption.

30 May 1677   At 37, marries a distant relation,
Catherine de Romanet, 25, in a celebrity-studded
ceremony. Catherine was worth 57,780 in capital,
Racine 56,000.

The Racines will have seven children: Jean-Baptiste
(1678), Marie-Catherine (1680), Anne (1682), Elizabeth
(1684), Jeanne-Françoise (1686), Madeleine (1688) and
Louis (1692). Jean-Baptiste will reject the diplomatic
career his father had mapped out, Louis will become a
writer and the girls will either marry or become nuns.

11 September 1677   Racine and Boileau are made
historiographers to the king, each receiving a
gratification of 6000 *livres* and the 'order' to produce
'diverse works' commanded by Louis XIV for his
greater glory. They are made members of the
Académie des inscriptions.

After years of following Louis about the battlefield,
Racine will produce *Eloge historique du Roy sur ses conquêtes
de 1672 à 1678* (1684) and a technical manual, *Relation
de ce qui s'est passé au siège de Namur* (1692).

2 January 1680 A mandate is issued for Racine's arrest in 'The Poison Affair' but the mandate is quashed from on high. No actual evidence against Racine ever surfaces.

1683 The Court settles permanently at Versailles and Racine eventually has his own apartment there (1695); he also scores a room at the exclusive Chateau de Marley where Louis XIV likes to hunt with his favourite dogs.

1685 On the death of Colbert, Racine writes *Idylle sur la Paix,* set to music by Lully and performed at Court.

1687 Racine brings out a second edition of *Oeuvres Complètes,* including *Phèdre* (Hippolytus is dropped from the title).

1688 *Esther,* an operatic play about the extermination of the Jews, is commissioned by Madame de Maintenon, for Saint-Cyr, the school for girls she founded.

1689 *Athalie,* an anguished 'religious play', is the second and last of the commissions for Saint-Cyr. It is attacked by the ever-vigilant cabal.

December 1690 Racine gets a cut-rate post as 'gentilhomme ordinaire du roi'.

8 April 1692 Racine and Boileau are awarded pensions, the last to be offered as funds dry up due to war and famine. Racine gets 4,000 p.a. – 2,000 more than the housebound Boileau – to defray his costs in keeping up with the king.

He moves his family to the dingily aristocratic rue des Marais-Saint-Germain (now Visconti). Racine's library contains 1736 books, many very valuable. His landlady and several neighbours are Jansenists and Racine helps negotiate a détente between the sect and the government.

1693   His post as 'gentilhomme ordinaire' is made hereditary.

1694   Racine's four *Cantiques spirituels* are sung before the king and included in a new edition of the *Oeuvres complètes*.

February 1695   Buys an extravagant 60,000 franc post as 'conseiller secrétaire du roi' in a fund-raising exercise of the king's – his one and only bad financial move.

Now firmly established as Louis XIV's preferred reader.

1697   Brings out his fourth and final *Oeuvres complètes* while secretly writing *Abrégé de l'Histoire de Port-Royal*, a 200-page history of the Jansenists.

Spring 1698   Racine falls seriously ill with a cold, rheumatism and food poisoning; in fact, he has liver cancer. He adds a codicil to his will stipulating that he be buried with the Jansenists at Port-Royal at the foot of his old science teacher, Dr Hamon.

21 April 1699   Racine dies at home in the rue Visconti, after receiving the last sacraments. Louis XIV remarks to Boileau: 'We certainly have lost something, you and I, in losing poor old Racine', and bestows pensions of 1000 francs each on the widow and the elder son.

PHEDRA

Racine's Preface to *Phèdre* (1677)

Here is another tragedy whose subject has been taken
from Euripides. Although I have arrived at the action
following a slightly different path from the one taken by
that author, I have enriched my play at every turn with
all that seemed to me most striking in his. If I owed him
the idea alone of Phedra as a character, I would have to
say I was indebted to him for the most sensible thing
I ever put on stage. I am not surprised that the character
enjoyed such immense success in Euripides' day, or that it
still succeeds so hugely in our own century, since Phedra
has all the qualities Aristotle required of the tragic hero –
qualities apt to excite pity and terror. Phedra is neither
entirely guilty nor entirely innocent. Through her destiny
and the wrath of the gods, Phedra is involved in an illicit
passion that she is the first to be horrified by. She does
everything she can to overcome it. She would rather die
than declare it to anyone. And when she is forced to
reveal it, she speaks of it with such confusion that it is
clear that her crime is more a punishment of the gods
than anything springing from her will.

I have even been careful to make her a little less odious
than she is in the tragedies of the Ancients, where she
herself resolves to accuse Hippolytus. I felt calumny was a
little too base and too black to put it in the mouth of a
princess, one who, moreover, has such noble and virtuous

feelings. This baseness seemed more appropriate to a nurse who might have more of a slave's inclinations and yet who still only resorts to the false accusation to save her mistress' life and honour. Phedra goes along with it only because she is beside herself with mental turmoil; she swiftly determines afterwards to vindicate innocence and declare the truth.

In Euripides and Seneca, Hippolytus is accused of having actually raped his step-mother: *vim corpus tulit* ['My body has suffered his violence']. But here he is only accused of having intended to. I wanted to spare Theseus a vehemence that might have made him less acceptable to the audience. As for Hippolytus as a character, I noticed with the Ancients that Euripides was attacked for having represented him as a philosopher-prince exempt from all imperfection – which meant the young man's death caused more indignation than pity. I felt I should give him some flaw that would make him slightly culpable in relation to his father without, however, detracting in any way from the greatness of soul whereby he preserves Phedra's honour and allows himself to be condemned without accusing her. I call a flaw the passion he feels in spite of himself for Aricia, who is the daughter and sister of mortal enemies of his father.

The character Aricia is not an invention of mine. Virgil says that Hippolytus married her and had a son by her after Asclepius brought him back to life. And I have also read further in certain authors that Hippolytus married and brought to Italy a young Athenian woman of noble birth who was called Aricia and who gave her name to a small town in Italy.

I cite these authorities because I am most scrupulously keen to follow the fable. I have even followed Theseus' history as it appears in Plutarch.

It is in this historian that I found that what gave rise to the belief that Theseus had gone down into the Underworld to kidnap Proserpina was a journey the prince had undertaken in Epirus, close to the source of the Acheron, to the home of a king whose wife Pirithous wanted to abduct and who held Theseus prisoner after bringing about Pirithous' death. In this way I tried to preserve the plausibility of the historical tale without shedding any of the ornamentation of the fable which so greatly enhances the poetry. And the rumour of Theseus' death, based on this legendary journey, gives Phedra space to make a declaration of love that becomes one of the principle causes of her calamity and which she would never have dared make as long as she believed her husband to be alive.

For the rest, I don't dare yet claim this play actually to be the best of my tragedies. I leave to my readers and to time to decide its true worth. What I can say is that I have never written a tragedy where virtue is made more abundantly clear as in this one. The smallest sins are severely punished. The mere thought of a criminal act is regarded with as much horror as the act itself. The weaknesses engendered by love are shown for what they are: real weaknesses. Passions are only paraded before our eyes in order to show all the chaos they cause; and vice is here depicted everywhere in colours that lead to understanding of and hatred for its moral ugliness. This is properly speaking the goal which any man who works for the public should set himself; and it is what was uppermost in the minds of the original poet-tragedians. Their theatre was a school where virtue was taught no less rigorously than in the schools of the philosophers. Aristotle strove accordingly to provide the rules of the dramatic poem; and Socrates, the wisest of the philosophers, was not above having a hand in the tragedies of Euripides. It is earnestly to be hoped that our works prove as solid and as full of useful instruction as those of these poets. This would perhaps provide a means for reconciling tragedy to a great many persons celebrated for their piety and their knowledge who have in recent times condemned it and who would no doubt judge it more favourably if authors thought as much of instructing their audience as of entertaining them – following thereby tragedy's real intention.

Characters

THESEUS, *King of Athens, son of Aegeus*

PHEDRA, *wife of Theseus, daughter of Minos and Pasiphae*

HIPPOLYTUS, *son of Theseus and Antiope, Queen of the Amazons*

ARICIA, *Blue-blood princess of Athens*

THERAMENES, *Hippolytus' governor*

OENON, *Phedra's nurse and confidante*

ISMEN, *Aricia's confidante*

PANOPE, *one of Phedra's attendants*

GUARDS

The scene is Troezen, a town in the Pelopponese.

A 'Guide to the Pronunciation of Names' will be found on page 85.

ACT ONE

Scene i – HIPPOLYTUS, THERAMENES

HIPPOLYTUS

It's decided, Theramenes; I'm leaving.
I can't go on here in this lovely place.
I'm shaking with this terrible doubt I'm in,
And when I think how idle I've become I'm ashamed.
I haven't seen my father for six months.
I don't know what's happened to him.
I don't even know where he is.

THERAMENES

And where do you propose to look, my Lord?
I understand your fear;
I've already searched the seas on either side of Corinth;
I've asked for Theseus along the banks of the Acheron,
Where it winds down into the kingdom of the dead;
I've been to Elis, and round Cape Tenaros,
As far as the sea that saw Icarus fall.
What new hope makes you think you'll find him,
And where; in which happy, unknown land?
Who knows, even, who knows if the King your father
Would like the reasons for his absence revealed?
Maybe, while we're all fretting over him,
Our hero's blissfully ensconced with some new paramour,
And wouldn't exactly like his wife . . .

HIPPOLYTUS

Dear Theramenes, stop; give Theseus his due.
He isn't like that anymore, and whatever's
Holding him it's not some whore.
Phedra fixed his wandering eye on her:
She fears no rival.
Looking for him, I'd only be doing my duty anyway,
And I'd be escaping from a place where I don't dare
    stay.

THERAMENES

Since when has this peaceful place frightened you,
    my Lord?
As a child you loved it.
You used to prefer it here to the
Noisy pomp of Athens and the court.
What danger, what anguish, is driving you away?

HIPPOLYTUS

Those happy days are gone. Everything's changed
Since the Gods sent to Troezen's shores
The daughter of Minos and Pasiphae.

THERAMENES

I understand: I know what upsets you.
The very sight of Phedra here hurts your eyes.
The moment she laid eyes on you
She had you exiled, evil step-mother that she is.
But her hatred, though focused on you then,
Has now either gone soft or evaporated.
And besides, what can you have to fear
From a dying woman, a woman who wants to die?

How could Phedra, ravaged by some disease she's
    determined to conceal,
Finally sick of herself and of the light of day,
Possibly do you harm?

HIPPOLYTUS

Her pointless hatred's not what I'm afraid of.
I'm escaping from a different enemy:
I'm fleeing, if you must know, this Aricia,
Sole survivor of the doomed family who were sworn
    to destroy us.

THERAMENES

So you wish to persecute her as well, my Lord?
What did the sweet sister
Ever have to do with her evil brothers' schemes?
Or is it her very innocence you hate?

HIPPOLYTUS

If I hated her, I wouldn't run away.

THERAMENES

My Lord, I'll tell you why you're running.
Could it be that the mighty Hippolytus,
Implacable enemy of the laws of love
And of the yoke that Theseus has so often worn,
    has vanished?
Venus, by you so long despised, has
In the end, perhaps, come out on Theseus' side?
Putting you on the same level as mere mortals,
She's forcing you, perhaps, to worship at her shrine?
You aren't in love, are you, my Lord?

HIPPOLYTUS
                              That's far enough!
My friend, you've known my heart since the day I first
    drew breath.
How can you imply I could betray
The feelings of a heart so proud, so scornful of love?
My mother was an Amazon; I sucked this pride that
Astounds you from her breast.
When I was older and wiser,
I congratulated myself on who I knew I was.
You were always devoted to me,
And told me the story of my father's life.
You know how my soul was lifted by your voice
And soared with the tales of his daring exploits.
You described this intrepid hero
Consoling the human race for Hercules' disappearance,
Monsters slaughtered and brigands put to death,
Procrustes, Cercyon, Sciron, and Sinis,
The giant of Epidaurus' scattered bones,
Crete smoking with the blood of the Minotaur.
But then you recited less glorious deeds:
Promises of eternal love offered everywhere and
    everywhere believed;
Helen abducted from her parents' home in Sparta;
Salamis looking on as Periboea wept;
Dozens of others whose names he's forgotten,
Trusting souls, every one of them deceived:
Ariadne telling her woes to the rocks of Naxos;
Only Phedra, in the end, was abducted into marriage . . .
You remember how I hated hearing it
And hurried you up,
Desperate to obliterate

The ugly side of such a wonderful story!
Do you think I'd now let myself be shackled too?
Would the Gods humiliate me that much?
Theseus' glorious deeds excuse his promiscuity;
My feeble sighs would make me all the more
   contemptible.
I've killed no monsters yet,
And have no right to falter like him.
And even if my pride yielded,
Would I choose Aricia to conquer me?
How could I forget
The eternal family feud that keeps us apart?
My father has damned her, and forbids her,
By severe laws, from marrying and bearing children.
Fearing a new shoot from a rotten tree,
He intends to bury the family name along with her.
A captive in his custody till she goes to the grave,
Wedding torches will never light her way.
Should I take up her cause against my vengeful father?
Set an example of filial revolt?
Waste my youth on a hopeless love . . .

THERAMENES

                              Why fight it, my Lord?
The gods aren't interested in what we think.
Theseus has opened your eyes by trying to keep them
   closed.
His hatred has fanned a rebel flame
Whose light makes his enemy shine.
But why be frightened of a love that's pure?
If it seems sweet, why not try it?
Do you still have some primitive inhibition?

Are you afraid to follow in Hercules' footsteps?
Venus managed to conquer his heart.
You fight her, but where would you be
If Antiope had kept on resisting and not
Burned with love for Theseus?
But all this talk's beside the point:
Admit it, things have changed; for some time now
We haven't seen you, proud and wild,
Flying in a chariot along the shore,
Or breaking in some indomitable stallion
With the skill you learned at Neptune's knee.
The forests ring less often with your cries;
Your eyes are heavy and smoulder with a secret flame.
No doubt about it: it's love, you're on fire;
You're wasting away with longing and trying not to
    show it.
So the bewitching Aricia has found the way to your
    heart?

HIPPOLYTUS
    Theramenes, I'm leaving. I must find my father.

THERAMENES
    Won't you see Phedra before you go,
    My Lord?

HIPPOLYTUS
            I intend to: please let her know.
    Since duty demands it, I'll see her.
    But what's troubling her precious Œnon now?

Scene ii – HIPPOLYTUS, ŒNON, THERAMENES

ŒNON

Troubling, my Lord? No-one could be as troubled as me.
The Queen's not long for this world.
In vain I've watched her night and day:
She's dying before my very eyes and will not tell me
    why.
Some madness drives her,
Won't let her sleep; it drags her out of bed.
She wants to get up and see the sun; and in her agony,
Orders me to shut everyone out . . .
She's coming.

HIPPOLYTUS

                    That's it. I'll go – I'll get out of her way.
She won't want to see a face she loathes.

Scene iii – PHEDRA, ŒNON

PHEDRA

This is far enough. Let's stay here, dear Œnon.
I can't go on: my strength's abandoned me.
The light hurts my eyes. So bright!
My legs are giving way.
Oh God!

She sits.

ŒNON

       May our tears placate you, almighty Gods!

PHEDRA

These trinkets, these veils weigh me down!
What meddling fool swept up my hair
Like this?
Everything
Overwhelms me, destroys me, conspires to destroy me.

ŒNON

See how hot and cold you blow!
It was you, you gave up your morbid plan,
You whipped us into doing you up;
You got your strength back,
You wanted to show yourself and to see the sun.
There it is, Madam, so now you want to hide yourself
   away again.
Can't you bear the light you were so desperate to see?

PHEDRA

Great Sun, shining creator of a doomed race,
You whose daughter my mother claimed to be,
Appalled as you must be at how you see me now,
Let me look upon you one last time.

ŒNON

Stop! Can't you give up this horrible idea?
How long do I have to watch you, renouncing life,
Preparing the grim rituals of death?

PHEDRA

God! If only I was sitting in the shade of the forest.

If only I could see, through a haze of golden dust,
A chariot hurtling along the track!

ŒNON

What was that, Madam?

PHEDRA

Talking to myself! Where am I? What did I say?
Where have I let my longing carry me?
My mind's gone: the Gods have stolen it away.
Œnon, my face is red with shame:
I've let you see too much of what's destroying me.
I can't help it, my eyes are filled with tears.

ŒNON

Don't! If you must blush, blush for this silence
That's making you so much worse.
You push us away, you won't listen.
Do you want to end your days unmourned?
What insanity makes you want to end your life?
What evil spell, what poison has sapped you at the
    source?
Darkness has shrouded the skies three times
Since you last slept;
The sun has hunted the night three times
Since you last ate.
What's got into you? What's wrong?
What right do you have to take your own life?
You offend the Gods who created you;
You betray your husband to whom you're bound by
    sacred vows;
You betray your poor, unhappy children,
Delivering them into slavery.

Remember: the same act that robs them of their mother
Offers the son of that foreign woman hope -
Your enemy, the enemy of your race,
The son that Amazon carried in her womb,
Hippolytus . . .

PHEDRA

Oh, God!

ŒNON

I've touched a raw nerve.

PHEDRA

You miserable creature, what name did you say?

ŒNON

Good! And so you should be angry!
I'm glad to see you tremble at that fatal name.
Live, then. Let love or duty goad you on.
Live, don't let that barbarous Scythian's son
Crush your children under his great boot and so
    command
The foremost race of Greece and of the gods.
But be quick about it: every breath brings you closer
    to death.
Pull yourself together.
Though the light within you is flickering,
It's still alight, it can still burst into flame.

PHEDRA

I've let it burn too long already.

ŒNON

What is it? What have you got to feel guilty about?

What have you done that's ripping you apart?
Are your hands dripping with innocent blood?

PHEDRA

My hands are clean.
Would to God my heart was!

ŒNON

What hideous scheme have you hatched
That's making you so wretched?

PHEDRA

I've said enough. Spare me.
I'd rather die than make such a fatal confession.

ŒNON

Die, then. Keep your cruel silence;
But find some other hand to close your eyes.
Though you're fading fast
I'll go down to the dead before you.
There are a hundred ways of getting there -
I'm so unhappy I'll find the shortest way.
You're so cruel; when have I ever failed you?
I nursed you when you were a babe in arms.
For you, I gave up everything, my country, my own
    children.
Is this what I get for such devotion!

PHEDRA

What do you hope to gain with this violent outburst?
You'd shiver with horror if I broke my silence.

ŒNON

And what about the horror, God knows,
Of seeing you die before my eyes?

PHEDRA

If you knew my sin, and the fate that's crushing me,
I'd still die, and all the more guilty.

ŒNON

Madam, in the name of all the tears I've cried for you,
As I kneel here before you,
Release me please. Tell me. Don't keep me in the dark.

PHEDRA

That's what you want? Stand up.

ŒNON

                                        I'm listening.

PHEDRA

What in God's name do I say! Where do I start?

ŒNON

Stop trying to frighten me!

PHEDRA

How Venus can hate! How deadly her rage!
First, there was my mother: . . .
Love hurled my mother into the abyss!

ŒNON

Put that behind you, Madam; let silence
Forever blot out the memory.

PHEDRA

Then there was Ariadne, my sister, so unlucky in love.
You died by the sea where Theseus deserted you!

ŒNON

What are you trying to prove? What terrible despair
  suddenly
Pits you against your whole family?

PHEDRA

Since Venus wishes, of all my deplorable family,
I'm the last, and the saddest, to die.

ŒNON

For love?

PHEDRA

I show all the signs of love's insanity.

ŒNON

Who is it?

PHEDRA

You'll die of horror when you hear.
I love . . . I can't say his name without shivering . . .
I love . . .

ŒNON

                  Who?

PHEDRA

                  You know this Amazon's son,
This prince I myself have so long oppressed?

ŒNON

Hippolytus! My God!

PHEDRA

You said his name, not me.

ŒNON

    Heaven help us! My blood has turned to ice.
    What an outrage! You godforsaken race!
    Why did we have to sail to these infested shores?
    I curse the day we foundered on the rocks.

PHEDRA

    It goes back much further. I'd only just
    Been bound in holy matrimony to the son of Aegeus;
    My security, my happiness seemed assured.
    But then Athens revealed to me my incomparable
      enemy.
    There he was: I turned red, I turned pale at the sight
      of him.
    My dazed mind reeled,
    I couldn't see, I couldn't speak;
    My whole body went cold and burned.
    I felt the hand of Venus in the searing lust
    She's always used to torture us.
    I thought I could fight it with fervent prayer:
    I built her a temple with lavish decorations.
    Night and day I sacrificed to her and in the victims'
    Entrails I looked for a sign of my release.
    But nothing can cure an incurable love!
    There was no point burning incense at the altar.
    When my lips invoked the Goddess by name,
    It was Hippolytus I worshipped; I saw him everywhere,
    Even through the smoke, the stench;
    I offered up my life to a god I dared not name.
    I avoided him constantly. That was the hardest part!
    I saw him in his own father's face.
    In the end I denied my deepest feelings:

I forced myself to persecute him.
I played the malevolent, unforgiving step-mother
To rout the enemy I idolised.
I urged his exile, I didn't let up until they'd
Torn him from his father's loving arms.
I could breathe, again, Œnon, once he was gone.
I was calmer and the days went by.
Hiding heartache behind my duties as wife and mother
I brought up my children.
What for! There's no escape from destiny!
Theseus himself, my husband, brought me here to
    Troezen,
And again I saw the enemy I'd so carefully removed:
My wound was still raw, it bled again.
My passion's no longer burning hidden in my veins:
Venus has ripped her prey right open with her claws.
I know how terrible my sin is,
I hate my life, I loathe this passion.
I hoped, in dying, to preserve my honour intact,
And prevent my dark secret from coming to light:
I couldn't stand your crying, your carrying on;
I've told you everything, and I won't repent,
As long as you respect that I'm near death
And don't hinder me, don't blame me.
Stop trying to fan
This tiny flame that's only just alive.

Scene iv – PHEDRA, ŒNON, PANOPE

PANOPE

    I would like to keep this tragic news from you,
    Madam, but I can't.
    Death has robbed you of your invincible husband, ˙
    And you're the last to know.

ŒNON

    What are you saying, Panope?

PANOPE

               That the Queen in her ignorance
    Prays for Theseus' return in vain;
    That from ships now in the harbour,
    Hippolytus has just learned of his father's death.

PHEDRA

                        Oh God!

PANOPE

    In Athens they're divided over the choice of his successor.
    Some are for the Prince, your son,
    Madam; others, the lawless rabble,
    Support the foreign woman's son.
    Rumour even has it there's a brazen plot
    To put Aricia on the throne.
    I felt I had to warn you.
    Hippolytus is ready and about to sail for Athens.
    If he should appear in the middle of the riot,
    He'll win the mob – they're easily swayed.

ŒNON

    That will do, Panope. The Queen can hear you,
    She'll take account of what you say.

Scene v – PHEDRA, ŒNON

ŒNON

Madam, I'd given up persuading you to live;

I even imagined following you to the grave.

There was nothing more I could say to dissuade you.

But this last catastrophe compels you to take a different
    tack.

Your destiny's changed.

The King is no more, Madam; long live the Queen!

He leaves you a son who has only you –

A slave if he loses you, but if you live, a king.

Who can he turn to in his grief but you?

There'd be no-one to wipe away his tears,

And the Gods would hear his innocent cries

And make their sentence heavier.

Live, now you're no longer in the wrong:

Your love's like any normal love.

In dying, Theseus has severed the ties that bind

And that made your passion so heinous a crime.

You needn't be so afraid of Hippolytus now;

You can see him without feeling guilty.

Maybe, convinced you hate him,

He'll lead the uprising against you.

Show him how wrong he is, bend his heart to your will.

He should be king of these happy shores, Troezen is
    his inheritance.

But he knows the law bequeaths to your son

The mighty city Athena built.
You have a common natural enemy:
You must unite to fight Aricia.

PHEDRA

Very well, I'll take your advice!
I'll live, if you can bring me back to life,
And if the love of my grieving son
Can restore my weary soul.

ACT II

Scene i – ARICIA, ISMEN

ARICIA

Hippolytus has asked to see me here?
Hippolytus is looking for me, to say goodbye?
Ismen, is it true? It's not some trick?

ISMEN

Only to be expected now Theseus is dead.
Prepare to be surrounded by the countless
Souls that Theseus alienated.
Aricia, you're finally mistress of your fate:
You'll soon see all of Greece at your feet.

ARICIA

So it's not just a rumour, then, Ismen.
I'm no longer a slave, no longer have an enemy?

ISMEN

No, Madam, the Gods are no longer against you;
Theseus has gone to join your dead brothers' ghosts.

ARICIA

Do they know how he came to grief?

ISMEN

Unbelievable stories are doing the rounds.
They say that, unfaithful as usual, he was drowned
    at sea

Carrying off his latest lover.
They even say – it's all over town –
He went down into Hades with his bosom friend
    Pirithöus,
Saw the river Cocytus and its sombre shores,
And showed himself living to the spirits of the dead.
But no-one comes back across that shore
And he's trapped with the dead for ever.

ARICIA

But how can a mortal, before their hour's up,
Penetrate the deep, distant house of the dead?
What magic lured him to those dreaded shores?

ISMEN

Theseus is dead, Madam. You're the only one who
    doubts it.
Athens mourns him. Troezen, knowing the facts,
Already claims Hippolytus as king.
Phedra is in the palace, trembling for her son,
And asking her distraught advisers what to do.

ARICIA

And you think Hippolytus will be kinder to me
Than his father was, and reduce my sentence?
Will he take pity on me?

ISMEN

                         Madam, I think he will.

ARICIA

You don't know how unfeeling Hippolytus can be!
What giddy hope makes you think he'll pity me,
Respect in me alone the sex he so despises?

You see for yourself how he's been avoiding us;
He only goes where he knows we won't be.

ISMEN

I know what a cold fish he's supposed to be,
But I've seen the high and mighty Hippolytus in your
     presence;
I've watched him closely – his reputation for aloofness
     I admit
Increased my curiosity.
Ice is not what I saw:
As soon as you looked at him he went to water,
He melted, he couldn't take his eyes off you,
No matter how he tried.
The term 'lover' may offend his famous pride,
But his eyes give him away, even if he doesn't know
     what to say.

ARICIA

Darling Ismen, your words are music to my ears,
But they may be unfounded.
You know me; could it be the sad plaything
Of a merciless fate,
A heart always fed on bitterness and tears,
Could come to feel the bitter-sweet torments of love?
Last of a royal dynasty, descended from the Earth,
I alone escaped the ravages of war.
I lost six brothers, mown down by Theseus in their
     prime . . .
The pride and joy of such an illustrious line!
They were lopped by the sword, every one, and the
     soaking earth
Sadly drank Erechtheus' royal blood.

As you know, since they died, a harsh law
Forbids all Greeks to marry me:
They're afraid one day my children would burn with
    my brothers'
Fearless flame
And renew the war.
But you know, too, how contemptuous I've been
Of our nervous conqueror's precautions.
I swore from the start I'd never love
And was grateful to Theseus in his tyranny
For steeling my resolve.
At the time, I had not yet . . . not yet seen his son.
Not that I like – love – only what I see, heaven forbid,
Though I appreciate his beauty, his celebrated grace,
Those abundant gifts of nature
He disdains, or seems not to know he has.
I love in him, I value, richer treasures:
His father's virtues, without his father's faults.
I love, I must admit, that regal pride
That's never been broken in by love.
Phedra prides herself on capturing a pushover.
No easy victory for me, I'm far prouder:
What's the good of homage offered everywhere,
What good is winning a heart that keeps being won?
But to storm a heart that's a fortress,
To wound a heart that won't feel pain,
To fetter a prisoner with chains he can't believe,
And watch him straining against the yoke he craves:
That's what I want; that's what I long for.
It'd be easier to tackle Hercules.
But then: 'sooner overcome, more often conquered'.
Where's the glory in that?

Oh, but darling Ismen, how conceited of me
When I'm sure to meet with solid resistance.
No doubt you'll hear me, humbled by heartache,
Moaning about the same pride that dazzles me today.
Hippolytus in love? As though I'd be so lucky.
Why should I succeed in breaking . . .

ISMEN

                                    Find out for yourself:
He's here to see you.

Scene ii – HIPPOLYTUS, ARICIA, ISMEN

HIPPOLYTUS

                              Madam, before leaving
I felt I should clarify your situation.
My father is no longer with us.
My premonition was correct:
I knew why he was gone so long.
Death alone could bring his amazing career to an end
And keep him so long hidden.
The Gods have finally let Death
Take him, Hercules' companion and heir.
I'm sure you'll allow him his virtues,
Even though you hate him,
And can hear all this without flinching.
For me one happy consequence softens the blow:
I can now release you and revoke
Those laws whose severity I deplored.

You are free to marry, to give your heart where you will;
Troezen, once the home of my ancestors,
And which I inherit today,
Elects me unanimously as king:
I leave you as free, no, freer than I am.

ARICIA

Your generosity is boundless, overwhelming.
To honour my disgrace with such kind concern,
My Lord, don't you see, is to put me in your debt,
As much as the laws from which you free me.

HIPPOLYTUS

Athens, faltering in its choice of a successor,
Speaks of you, of me, of the son of the Queen.

ARICIA

Me, Sir?

HIPPOLYTUS

     I know, I'm well aware that
The unjust laws of Athens would seem to eliminate me:
Greece won't forgive me for my foreign mother.
But if my brother, Phedra's son, were my only rival,
Madam, I could certainly defend my rights
Against the capriciousness of the law.
Something more deserving
Stops me from pressing my claim.
I must hand over to you, or rather, hand back,
The sceptre your ancestors once received
From Earth's most famous son.
It was placed in Aegeus' hands by adoption.
My father, his son, expanded Athens, protected her
And was therefore joyfully acclaimed as king,

And your poor brothers were consigned to oblivion.
Athens calls you back now within its walls.
She has lost too much blood in this endless, futile feud;
For too long your butchered race has lain in furrows,
Blood and bone for the fuming fields.
Troezen is now under my command. The countryside
   of Crete
Offers Phedra's son a rich retreat,
But Attica belongs to you. I'm leaving, and on your
   behalf,
Will unite the votes divided between us.

ARICIA

I can't believe my ears.
I almost feel, I feel I'm dreaming.
Am I awake? Can I believe you're serious?
What God, what immortal has inspired you?
No wonder they sing your praises wherever you go.
The reality far exceeds the legend!
So you would betray your own interests, then, for me?
It would have been enough not to hate me,
To have been able to defend your heart so long
Against such enmity . . .

HIPPOLYTUS

                    Me, hate you, Madam?
However fierce they've made me out to be,
Do you think I'm some monster's son?
How savage one would have to be, how sunk in hate,
To be able to look at you, and not melt?
How could I resist your bewitching . . .

ARICIA
   Oh, my Lord.

HIPPOLYTUS
                    I've gone too far.
   I see I can't control my emotions.
   Since I've broken my silence
   Madam, I must go on: I must tell you
   The secret my heart can no longer contain.
   You see before you a pitiable prince,
   The very image of fearless pride.
   I spurned the whole idea of love,
   Offended by its captives and their chains;
   Pitying the wrecks of flesh and blood,
   I always thought to watch the storm from the shore.
   Now I'm like all the rest,
   I see myself swept out to sea!
   I was defeated in a moment:
   My proud spirit is finally brought to heel;
   For six months, ashamed, in despair,
   Pierced by an arrow,
   I've raged against you, against myself.
   It's no use.
   When you're there, I run away;
   When you're not, I see you
   Everywhere;
   Deep in the forest, your image haunts me;
   By day, by night,
   Everything shines with your radiance;
   I would rebel, I can't;
   Everything makes me your slave.
   I don't recognise myself; I'm lost.

My bow, my spears, my chariot – I despise them;
I've forgotten what it was that Neptune taught me.
The woods ring only with my lovesick sighs,
My stallions stand idle – they've forgotten the sound
   of my voice.
You must be appalled at this declaration,
To have aroused such savage love!
How could I offer you my heart in such brutal terms!
Don't you find your prisoner bizarre?
All the more reason to value my love – it's genuine.
Remember, I'm speaking a foreign language;
Don't reject what I'm saying because I don't know how
   to say it;
Without you, I'd never have felt what I feel.

Scene iii

HIPPOLYTUS, ARICIA, THERAMENES, ISMEN

THERAMENES
   The Queen is coming, my Lord. I ran ahead.
   It's you she wants to see.

HIPPOLYTUS
                          Me?

THERAMENES
                                    I know nothing.
   Phedra's sent for you.
   She wants to talk to you before you go.

HIPPOLYTUS

Phedra? What will I tell her? What can she hope to
hear . . .

ARICIA

Hear her out, my Lord. Let her speak.
She may have been your bitter enemy
But you owe her tears some pity.

HIPPOLYTUS

Meanwhile you're leaving. And I'm setting sail.
And I don't know
If I've offended the woman I adore!
I don't know if the heart I leave in your hands . . .

ARICIA

Go, Prince, and carry out your noble plan.
Bring Athens under my control.
I accept the gifts you shower on me.
But ultimately the whole vast, glorious empire
Is not, of all your presents, the one I cherish most.

Scene iv – HIPPOLYTUS, THERAMENES

HIPPOLYTUS

Is everything ready, my friend? Oh, the Queen's here.
Go – make sure we're ready to sail.
Give the signal, run, then hurry back
And rescue me from this ill-timed encounter.

Scene v – PHEDRA, HIPPOLYTUS, ŒNON

PHEDRA,
    He's here. My blood's all rushed to my heart.
    Now I see him I forget what I came to say.

ŒNON
    Don't forget your son – you're his only hope.

PHEDRA
    I hear you're leaving us, rather suddenly,
    My Lord. I've come to add my tears to your grief.
    I've come to tell you my fears for my son.
    My son's also lost his father; and the day's not far off
    When he'll have to face my death as well.
    Even now countless enemies are preying on his youth.
    Only you can protect him.
    But a secret remorse is nagging me.
    I fear I've made you deaf to my son's cries;
    I shudder to think that in your righteous anger
    You'll attack in him his odious mother.

HIPPOLYTUS
    Madam, I wouldn't stoop so low.

PHEDRA
    If you did hate me, my Lord, I could hardly complain,
    You've seen me bent on destroying you;
    But you couldn't see what was at the bottom of my
        heart.

I did everything I could to earn your hatred.
I couldn't stand your breathing the same air, on the
    same shores.
Publicly, privately, declaring myself against you,
I put the sea between us.
I even made it a crime, punishable by law,
For your name to be spoken in my presence.
But if the punishment should fit the crime,
If hate alone can attract hate,
No woman ever deserved pity more
Or less deserved, my Lord, your rage.

HIPPOLYTUS

A mother jealous of her children's rights
Rarely forgives the son of a previous wife.
I realise this, Madam. Nagging suspicions
Are the commonest offspring of second marriages.
Anyone would have been just as jealous in your place;
I might have come off far worse.

PHEDRA

Oh, no, my Lord! I swear the Gods
Have made me the exception to the rule!
I'm disturbed, devoured by something quite rare!

HIPPOLYTUS

Madam, it's too soon to wear black, I know.
Your husband might still be alive;
Heaven may bring him back in answer to our prayers.
Neptune watches over him
And won't let his prayers go unheard.

PHEDRA

No-one crosses death's river twice,

My Lord. Since Theseus set eyes on those sinister
   shores,
You hope in vain some God will send him back;
The greedy Acheron never lets go of its prey.
Why do I say that? He isn't dead; he lives in you.
I seem always to see my husband before me.
I see him, I talk to him; and my heart . . . I'm raving,
My Lord, I can't hold back this mad passion.
There's nothing I can do.

HIPPOLYTUS

   Your love is extraordinary:
   You still see Theseus, although he's dead.
   Your soul still burns with love for him.

PHEDRA

   Yes, Prince, I burn for Theseus.
   I love him, not as he's been in the Underworld,
   A fickle philanderer with a roving eye,
   Bringing disgrace to the God of Hades' bed;
   But loyal, lofty, and a bit fierce,
   Charming, young, trailing hearts wherever he goes,
   The way they depict the Gods, or as I see you before me.
   He had your bearing, your eyes, your way of talking,
   The same noble reticence put colour in his cheeks.
   He sailed through the waves into Crete,
   A fine specimen for the daughters of Minos to love.
   Where were you then? Why, without Hippolytus,
   Did he seem to be the cream of Greece's heroes?
   Why – you weren't old enough – but why couldn't you
   Have been on the ship that sent him to our shores?
   You would have slaughtered the Minotaur, our monster
      half-brother,

Despite all the twists and turns of his endless Labyrinth;
My sister would have armed you with her fatal thread
And led you through the dizzying maze.
No – I would have beaten her to it;
Love would have shown me what to do.
I, I alone, Prince, would have come to your rescue,
   helped you
Negotiate the Labyrinth's entanglements.
How I would have improvised, for that gorgeous face!
A miserable thread wouldn't have done *me*.
I'd have stood beside you in the danger you faced,
No – I'd have gone first.
I'd have gone down into the Labyrinth with you
And emerged with you later, or been lost.

HIPPOLYTUS

My God, Madam, aren't you forgetting
Theseus is my father, and your husband?

PHEDRA

And what makes you think I've forgotten,
Prince? Do you think I'm now past caring?

HIPPOLYTUS

I'm sorry, Madam. I'm so embarrassed -
Obviously I've misinterpreted you
Without meaning to.
I'm so ashamed, I can't look at you;
I must go . . .

PHEDRA

                    So cruel! You understood me alright.
I went too far for you to get it wrong.
So be it! Know Phedra, then, in all her insane passion!

I love you. Don't think for a moment I'm innocent in
   my own eyes,
Pleased with myself for loving you.
Don't think cowardly complacency has fostered the
   poisonous love
That's destroying my sanity.
Cursed victim of the Gods' revenge,
I abhor myself far more than you can hate me.
The Gods are my witness, those same Gods who've
   branded me
With the deadly lust that burns my race to cinders;
The Gods who've taken such delight
In making me depraved.
Try remembering:
I didn't just shun you, I had you thrown out.
I wanted to seem abominable, inhuman to you;
If I got you to hate me, it was the better to resist you.
What was the use?
You hated me more, I loved you no less.
Your hardships only made me want you more.
I languished, I wilted, on fire, in tears.
You would've seen,
If you could've brought yourself to look at me.
Why am I saying this? You don't think I meant to
   tell you
What I've just confessed!
Trembling for a son I could not betray,
I came to you to beg you not to hate him.
Any excuse for a heart that's bursting!
But I can't talk about anyone but you.
Take your revenge, punish me for a love you loathe.
Prove yourself your father's son and

Rid the world of a monster who appals you.
Theseus' widow dares to love his son!
Believe me, you musn't let so monstrous a mother
   get away.
Here is my heart. Stab me, here.
My heart's busting to atone for its sins,
I can feel it rising to meet your blade.
Put it in! If you think my heart's beneath you,
If you think it's too sweet a way for me to go, or
Your hand would be contaminated by such wicked blood,
Forget it. Give me the sword.
Give it to me.

ŒNON

                    What are you doing, Madam? God help us!
Someone's coming. Don't let them see you.
Come, let's go back, avoid disgrace.

Scene vi – HIPPOLYTUS, THERAMENES

THERAMENES

Is that Phedra running away, or being dragged?
My Lord, are you in pain?
I find you swordless, speechless, white as a ghost.

HIPPOLYTUS

Theramenes, we must flee. Something terrible's
   happened.
I can't look at myself without horror.

Phedra . . . No, no, Almighty Gods! Let her horrible secret
  Sink without a trace.

THERAMENES
  If you're ready to leave, the ships are waiting.
  But Athens, my Lord, has already declared itself.
  The votes are counted:
  Your brother's won, Phedra is in power.

HIPPOLYTUS
  Phedra?

THERAMENES
      A herald from Athens
  Has just placed the reins of power in her hands.
  Her son, my Lord, is king.

HIPPOLYTUS
             You Gods, who know her,
  Is this a reward for her virtue, then?

THERAMENES
  However, there's a rumour that the King's still alive.
  They claim Theseus has been seen in Epirus.
  But I looked for him there, so I know . . .

HIPPOLYTUS.
  Doesn't matter. Let's leave no stone unturned.
  We'll investigate the rumour, trace it to its source.
  If it's not worth holding up the voyage,
  We'll go; and whatever it costs,
  We'll place the sceptre in hands worthy of receiving it.

ACT III

Scene i – PHEDRA, ŒNON

PHEDRA

Oh, let them take their honours elsewhere!
Stop interfering! Why do you want people to see me?
Why are you trying to delude me?
You'd be better off keeping me hidden: I've said too
    much already.
My wild desire spilled over in public.
I said what should never have been heard.
God! How he took it in!
How he tried to evade my meaning!
How furious he was to get away!
He went so red my shame was overwhelming!
Why did you save my life?
Oh, God! When his sword was pointing at my heart,
Did he go pale, did he tear it from my hands?
All I had to do was lightly touch it,
And it became hideous in his inhuman eyes;
This miserable piece of tin now stains his hands.

ŒNON

All you can do is feel sorry for yourself,
Fanning the fire you ought to put out.
Wouldn't it be better, as Minos' worthy daughter,
To seek peace in higher concerns?

Turn your back on that good-looking, ungrateful brat,
Rule and immerse yourself in affairs of state.

PHEDRA

Me, rule! Me, make laws to run a state,
When my feeble reason no longer rules me!
When I've lost control of my senses!
When I can hardly breathe under the weight of this yoke!
When I'm dying!

ŒNON

Get away.

PHEDRA

I can't leave him.

ŒNON

You once dared banish him, now you don't dare leave
him alone.

PHEDRA

It's too late now. He knows I'm dying for him.
The bounds of decency have been crossed.
I declared myself guilty in front of my conqueror,
And hope, incredibly, has slipped into my heart.
When my life was hanging by a thread
You roused my failing strength.
You talked me round with lies.
You let me believe my love could be allowed.

ŒNON

Whether you're innocent or guilty,
There's nothing I wouldn't have done to save you.
But if insult could ever goad you into action,
Don't ever forget that arrogant young stallion's derision.

Did you see his cold, cruel eyes, his pigheaded
    self-righteousness,
The way he left you practically prostrate at his feet!
Stuck-up brat with his stupid pride!
If only you could've seen him then through my eyes!

PHEDRA

Œnon, he may outgrow this pride that so offends you.
He's as rough as the forest he was brought up in;
Poor, uncivilized Hippolytus has heard words of love
For the first time in his life.
Perhaps he was too shocked to speak.
I was too forceful, I went too far . . .

ŒNON

Remember, he was suckled at a savage breast.

PHEDRA

Savage she may have been, a barbarous Scythian,
But not incapable of love.

ŒNON

He hates our entire sex to death.

PHEDRA

Then I'll never be cast aside for some other woman.
All your good advice is now out of season.
Serve my passion, Œnon, and not my reason.
He fends off love with a heart that's unassailable.
Let's find a more vulnerable organ to attack.
The lure of empire seems to attract him;
He liked the idea of Athens, he couldn't disguise it.
His ships were already pointed in that direction,
Sails fluttering in the wind.

Œnon, track him down, our ambitious schemer,
Dangle the gleaming crown in front of his eyes.
Let him don the sacred diadem;
All I ask is the honour of putting it on him myself;
I'm happy to hand over power I can't hold.
He can teach my son the art of command.
He may even be glad to be a father to him.
From now on both son and mother are in his power.
Use any means you can to bring him round:
He'll listen to you, not me.
Entreat him, sob, groan; wail about how I'm fading fast;
Don't be ashamed to beg.
I'll take responsibility; you're my only hope,
Go to him: my life's in your hands.

Scene ii – PHEDRA, *alone*

Oh you, who see how far I've fallen,
Implacable Venus, have you humiliated me enough?
You couldn't be more cruel.
Your triumph is complete; all your arrows have hit home.
Cruel Goddess, if you're looking for further glory,
Pick on a more rebellious enemy.
Hippolytus shuns you and never worships at your shrine,
No matter how angry that may make you.
Your very name offends him.
Take revenge, Goddess . . . we share a common cause.

Make him love . . . Œnon, you're back?
He loathes me, he won't listen.

Scene iii – PHEDRA, ŒNON

ŒNON

You must stifle any thought, Madam, of this
   impossible love.
Resume your past virtue.
The King we thought was dead is on his way;
Theseus has reappeared, Theseus is here.
Everyone's pushing and shoving to get a glimpse of him.
I went out looking for Hippolytus, as instructed,
And the air was filled with shouting.

PHEDRA

My husband's alive, Œnon, say no more.
I've basely confessed to a love which must outrage him.
He's alive: I don't want to know any more.

ŒNON

What?

PHEDRA

I told you this would happen, but you wouldn't have it.
Your tears got the better of my remorse.
This morning I was dying; I would have been mourned.
I took your advice, and die disgraced.

ŒNON
    Die?

PHEDRA
        God help me! What have I done?
My husband's coming and his son with him.
I'll see the witness of my adulterous desires
Observe how brazenly I dare approach his father,
My heart heavy with sighs he refused to hear,
My eyes wet with tears the callous boy disdained.
Do you think he'll be concerned for Theseus' honour,
And keep quiet about the passion I feel?
Will he let his father and his king be betrayed?
Will he be able to contain the horror he feels for me?
His silence will be in vain. I know what I've done,
Œnon. I'm not one of those brazen women
Who commit adultery without blushing.
I know the savage force of my delirium, I recall every
    wild spasm.
I feel that these walls, these very roofs
Will find a voice; they're ready to accuse me,
Waiting for my husband to return to tell him all.
I wish I were dead.
May death deliver me from so many horrors.
Is it so dreadful to stop living?
For the desperate, death holds no fear.
I fear only for the reputation I leave behind.
What a legacy to bequeath my poor children!
Jupiter's royal blood should swell their pride;
But no matter how proud they manage to be,
The sins of the mother are a heavy burden.
I fear one day they'll be made to pay

For their mother's guilt.
I fear the weight will crush them.
How will they hold their heads up?

ŒNON

Yes, I pity them both.
You're right to be afraid.
But why leave them open to such attacks?
Why put yourself on trial?
You'll only lose: they'll say that Phedra, obviously guilty,
Fled in fear at the sight of the husband she deceived.
Lucky Hippolytus if you end your days
And thereby prove him right.
How could I fend off your accuser?
He'd easily refute me.
I'd have to watch him enjoying his horrible triumph,
Telling anyone who'll listen of your shame.
Oh, I'd rather the flames of hell devoured me!
But be honest, do you still love him?
How do you see your bold prince now?

PHEDRA

He's vile, a monster in my eyes.

ŒNON

So why let him get away with it?
You're afraid of him. Get in first: accuse him
Of the crime he might lay at your door this very day.
Who's going to contradict you? Everything speaks
    against him:
His sword left happily in your hands,
The state you're in now, your past resentment,

The way you warned his father long ago -
You already obtained his exile.

PHEDRA

Me, oppress and blacken innocence?

ŒNON

Keep your mouth shut. That's all you have to do.
Like you, I'm trembling, I'm sorry to have to do it,
I'd rather die a thousand deaths.
But if I don't resort to this, I'll lose you; and,
I love you more than anything in the world . . .
I'll do the talking. Enraged by what I reveal, Theseus
Won't go further than his son's exile.
A father, though he punishes, is still a father, Madam:
A mild sentence will satisfy his anger.
But even if innocent blood were shed,
What sacrifice doesn't your threatened honour demand?
It's too precious to be compromised.
Whatever it dictates, you must accept, Madam;
To save your honour
Everything, even virtue, must be sacrificed.
They're coming. I see Theseus.

PHEDRA

                              And I see Hippolytus!
In his insolent eyes I see written my doom.
Do what you will, I'm in your hands.
In the agony I'm in, I can do nothing for myself.

Scene iv

THESEUS, HIPPOLYTUS, PHEDRA, ŒNON,
THERAMENES

THESEUS

Fortune at last has smiled on me,
Madam; I return to your loving arms . . .

PHEDRA

Stop, Theseus, don't go on,
Don't profane such intimacy.
I no longer deserve your affection.
You've been gravely wronged.
In your absence jealous Fortune has not spared your wife.
I no longer deserve to please you, or even to be near you.
From now on my one thought must be to keep away.

Scene v – THESEUS, HIPPOLYTUS, THERAMENES

THESEUS

Strange welcome, son.
What does it mean?

HIPPOLYTUS

Only Phedra can shed light on that.
But if my fervent pleas can move you,
Permit me, my Lord, never to set eyes on her again.
Permit your trembling son
To vanish from the place your wife inhabits.

THESEUS

My son, you'd leave me?

HIPPOLYTUS

    I'm not the one who went looking for her:
    It's you who brought her to these shores.
    When you went off again, my Lord, you decided to bring
    Aricia and the Queen to Troezen;
    You even committed them to my care.
    But what obligations keep me here now you're back?
    I've thrown away my youth idling in the forest,
    Pitting my strength against puny enemies.
    Shouldn't I stop idly toying and
    Dip my spears in more glorious blood?
    You weren't even as old as I am now,
    Before many a tyrant, many a ferocious monster
    Had felt the weight of your arm.
    Already, gleefully dispensing justice,
    You'd rid the whole coast of pirates.
    The traveller felt protected, no longer feared assault;
    Hercules could breathe easy and rest on his laurels,
    Knowing you could now take over . . .
    But I'm the unknown son of such a glorious father;
    I haven't yet even caught up to my mother.
    At least let me show you what I'm made of.
    If some monster has somehow escaped you,
    Let me place its pelt at your feet to honour you,
    Or let the memory of an honourable death,
    Immortalise a life so nobly ended
    And prove to the world I was your son.

THESEUS

    What is this? What seeping horror has spread through
      this place
    And makes my family flee from me distraught?

If I was going to return so feared and unwanted,
Why did the Gods let me out of prison?
I had one friend. He became reckless with desire,
He wanted to carry off the tyrannical king of Epirus'
    queen.
Reluctantly I helped him in his amorous scheme,
But Destiny was outraged and blinded us.
The tyrant stole up on me when I was unarmed and
    defenceless.
I wept as I watched the barbarian deliver
Poor Pirithous to the vicious monsters he kept
And fed on the flesh of unlucky men.
Then he locked me up in a vast, dark cavern,
Deep down, near the kingdom of the dead.
Six months later, the Gods deigned to notice me:
I escaped under the warder's nose
And wiped out one of nature's worst mistakes.
His own monsters made a meal of him.
But when my heart leapt for joy
At returning to the ones I love,
And when I felt my very being
Restored by the sight of them,
They all run away in fear!
Should I be frightened of myself?
Perhaps I should have stayed
Locked up with the monsters in Epirus.
What's going on?
Phedra warns me I've been gravely wronged.
Who has betrayed me? Why haven't I been avenged?
Has Greece, which I've always protected,
Offered the criminal refuge?
You don't answer. Is my son, my own son,

Consorting with the enemy?
Let's go in. I've had enough of this.
I'll hear the crime and who is guilty.
Let Phedra explain the distress I see she's in.

Scene vi – HIPPOLYTUS, THERAMENES

HIPPOLYTUS

What did he mean by that – it made my blood run cold.
Phedra's still in the grip of frenzy,
Will she accuse herself and thereby hang herself?
God! What'll the King say? What deadly poison
Love has spread throughout the house!
Even me, full of the desire he condemns,
How different I am from what I was before!
Dark forebodings make my skin crawl.
But I'm innocent after all – I've got nothing to fear.
Come, I'll find another way to appeal
To my father's tenderer feelings.
I'll tell him of my love; he may try to interfere,
But he can never shake it.

ACT IV

Scene i – THESEUS, ŒNON

THESEUS
>   What are you telling me? This traitor, this strutting lout
>   Planned to destroy his father's honour?
>   Destiny, how relentlessly you hound me!
>   I don't know where I'm going, I don't know where I am.
>   All my tenderness! My goodness spat on!
>   What a hideous, hateful scheme!
>   To achieve the evil end of his illicit love,
>   The brute used force.
>   I recognised his sword, the same sword
>   I gave him for a nobler purpose.
>   Didn't all the ties of blood restrain him?
>   And why did Phedra put off punishing him?
>   Did she hope to spare him by keeping quiet?

ŒNON
>   No, Phedra was hoping to spare his unfortunate father.
>   Mortified by her lover's crazed designs
>   And the criminal fire in his eye,
>   Phedra was dying, my Lord, and would have put out
>   The light in her eyes by her own hand
>   If I hadn't seen her arm go up, and run to save her.
>   Only I could preserve her for your love;
>   I pitied both her distress and your alarm, and so
>   I've had to explain her tears; I didn't want to.

THESEUS

    The bastard! No wonder he went white!
    I noticed him jump with fear at my approach.
    I was stunned at how joyless he looked to see me;
    His stiff hug chilled me to the bone.
    But was this guilty love that's devouring him
    Already obvious in Athens?

ŒNON

    My Lord, you remember how the Queen used to
      complain.
    Now you know why.

THESEUS

    And then in Troezen the fire flared up again?

ŒNON

    I've told you, my Lord, all that happened.
    I've left the Queen too long on her own.
    Please let me hurry back to her.

Scene ii – THESEUS, HIPPOLYTUS

THESEUS

    Here he is! Ah, God! Who wouldn't be tricked
    By his noble bearing?
    How can a base adulterer like that
    Seem to glow with virtue?
    Shouldn't we be able to recognise a treacherous heart
    By unmistakable signs?

HIPPOLYTUS

    May I ask, my Lord, what dark cloud
    Hides your most august face?
    Won't you confide in your faithful son?

THESEUS

    Traitor! You dare show yourself to me?
    Monster! You should have been struck by lightning
        long ago!
    I must have missed you when I purged the earth
    Of the last of its vile scum!
    You dare show your face to me
    Here in this place you've polluted
    With your ghastly love – this lust
    That drove you as far as your own father's bed!
    Go! Crawl under a rock! Hide
    Somewhere far away
    Where no-one's heard of Theseus
    Or who he is, or what you are!
    Don't brave my hate again,
    Or tempt the fury I can barely contain.
    Fathering a son like you
    Has brought me shame enough
    Without your death tarnishing my memory,
    And dinting the glory of my noble deeds.
    Get right away, unless you want to die
    Like the other mongrel dogs I've happily dispatched.
    Take care the sun that lights our days
    Never catches you with your foot on this soil again.
    Go, I say; go as fast as you can, and never turn back,
    Purge my realm of your stinking presence.
    And you, Neptune, if I have, in the past,

Cleared your coasts of infamous assassins,
Remember, to reward a successful campaign,
You promised to grant my one most fervent wish.
In all the long hard months in prison
I never once called on you.
I saved your mercy for more pressing needs.
I implore you now, Neptune. Revenge a wronged father.
This traitor I abandon to your unremitting rage.
Quench the obscene fires in his blood.
I'll recognise your power by the fury of your revenge.

HIPPOLYTUS

Phedra accuses me of a criminal love!
Horror numbs my soul;
Unexpected blows rain down on me.
I can't breathe. My voice has dried up.

THESEUS

Traitor, you thought she'd be scared into silence
And this would bury your shameless brutality!
Pity that in your flight you left behind you, in her hands,
The sword that overwhelmingly condemns you!
You should have gone the whole way
And with one thrust silenced her and killed her.

HIPPOLYTUS

Justly provoked by so black a lie, my Lord,
I ought to now reveal the truth.
But I won't since it would hurt you.
Understand I'm keeping quiet out of respect for you;
Don't make things harder for yourself.
Look at my life, remember who I am.
Small crimes always precede great ones.

Whoever steps over the line drawn by the Law
Can end up violating the most sacred of all laws.
Like virtue, crime has its degrees;
And quivering innocence has never been seen
To swing suddenly to the opposite extreme.
A single day's not long enough to make a treacherous
    assassin,
An incestuous coward, of a virtuous man.
Breast-fed by an Amazon,
I've never betrayed my origins.
Pittheus, renowned for his wisdom,
Was kind enough to tutor me when I was off her hands.
I don't want to boast, my Lord,
But if I have any claim to virtue,
I believe I have demonstrated clearly how I hate
The evil acts they dare impute to me.
I've carried virtue to the limits of severity.
That's what I'm famous for in all of Greece.
My rigour, my austerity, are well known.
The day isn't purer than I am in my heart of hearts.
Yet, mad with lust, I'm supposed to have . . .

THESEUS

Yes, it's that very pride, you coward, that condemns you!
Now I see why you were so cold:
Only Phedra attracted your lascivious gaze;
You were indifferent, you refused to burn
With an innocent flame for anyone else.

HIPPOLYTUS

No, father. My heart, I won't deny it,
Has not refused to burn with a pure love.
On my knees I'll confess my real offence:

I love, it's true, I love, despite your prohibition;
Aricia rules my heart and mind; yes,
Your enemy's daughter has conquered your son.
I adore her and, in revolt against your express command,
My heart can only burn for her.

THESEUS

You love her? God, how transparent!
Confessing a crime to avoid judgement!

HIPPOLYTUS

My Lord, for six months I've avoided her,
But I love her.
I came, trembling, to tell you to your face.
God! Can't anything convince you you're wrong?
What dreadful solemn oath will reassure you?
Let the earth, the sky, the entire natural world . . .

THESEUS

Scoundrels always perjure themselves.
Please, spare me your little speech.
If that's all you have to prop up false virtue.

HIPPOLYTUS

To you it seems false, and full of tricks.
In her heart, Phedra does me greater justice.

THESEUS

Ah! Your insolence makes my blood boil!

HIPPOLYTUS

How long do you give me in exile, and where?

THESEUS
    Even if you were way beyond Hercules' gates
    I'd still feel I was too close to you, you swine.

HIPPOLYTUS
    Charged with the hideous crime you suspect me of,
    What friends will comfort me, if you abandon me?

THESEUS
    Go and find friends whose sick esteem
    Honours adultery, finds incest something to applaud;
    Traitors, lawless parasites with no sense of honour,
    Fit to protect the likes of you.

HIPPOLYTUS
    You can still talk of incest and adultery?
    I have nothing to say. Just this:
    Phedra is her mother's daughter;
    Her race, my Lord, as you well know,
    Is much more at home with all those horrors than mine.

THESEUS
    What! You'll stop at nothing?
    For the last time, vanish, traitor,
    Go. Don't wait for your furious father
    To have you dragged away in shame.

Scene iii – THESEUS, *alone*
    Miserable thing, you're going to your certain death.
    By the River Styx, which even the Gods fear,

Neptune gave me his word, and he'll keep it.
The God of Vengeance is at your heels, you can't escape.
I loved you once; and my heart already aches for you,
In spite of your offence.
But you forced me to sentence you to death.
Was any father ever so badly wronged?
Just Gods, you see the pain that's tearing me apart,
How can I have fathered such a monstrous child?

Scene iv – PHEDRA, THESEUS

PHEDRA

My Lord, I come to you in terror:
I heard your awesome voice
And fear your threat will instantly be carried out.
If there's still time, have mercy on your family.
Spare your flesh and blood, for pity's sake.
Save me from the horror of hearing his cries;
Don't make me pay with eternal agony
For having caused his own father to take his life.

THESEUS

You're wrong, Madam, my hand is not dripping with
    his blood.
The wretch hasn't escaped, though.
A divine hand has been charged with his destruction.
Neptune owes it to me; you will be revenged.

PHEDRA
     Neptune owes it to you! What! Your angry prayers . . .

THESEUS
     Why! Are you already afraid they'll be heard?
     Shouldn't you join me, instead, in my righteous prayers?
     Tell me everything he did in all its foulness.
     I'm too restrained, too slow – stir up my rage.
     And you don't know all he's capable of:
     His rage against you spills over in insults:
     He claims you lie with every breath;
     His heart, he maintains, and his fidelity, belong to Aricia,
     He loves her.

PHEDRA
                    What did you just say!

THESEUS
                         That's what he'd have me believe,
     As though I could be fooled so easily.
     Let Neptune act swiftly.
     I'll kneel again at his altar
     And urge him to keep his immortal word.

Scene v – PHEDRA, *alone*

     He's gone. My ears are ringing.
     My smouldering heart's on fire again!
     That's a bolt from the blue! Oh God! This news will
          kill me.

All I wanted was to save his son;
Driven by remorse,
I tore myself away from Œnon.
Who knows how far repentance would have made
    me go?
Perhaps I'd even have accused myself;
Perhaps, if my voice had held,
I'd have blurted out the hideous truth.
Hippolytus can feel, but he feels nothing for me!
His heart belongs to Aricia! He's faithful to Aricia!
God! When that ungrateful swine
Looked daggers at me,
I thought he'd turned his back on love
And hated all women equally.
But another woman has broken him.
In his cruel eyes, another woman has found favour.
Perhaps he's easily had, after all,
And I, I alone, disgust him.
And I feel I should defend him?

Scene vi – PHEDRA, ŒNON

PHEDRA
    Dear Œnon, do you know what I just heard?

ŒNON
    No, but I come to you trembling, I must say.
    When you rushed off, I felt faint:
    I was worried what your madness would make you say.

PHEDRA

Œnon, who'd have thought it? I had a rival.

ŒNON

What?

PHEDRA

Hippolytus is in love. I know for sure.
The fierce, untamable enemy of love,
That tiger I was always frightened to go near
Is now subdued, tamed; he acknowledges a conqueror:
Aricia has found the way to his heart.

ŒNON

Aricia?

PHEDRA

Oh! This particular pain is new to me!
What other torments do I have in store!
All I've gone through, fear and frenzy,
The fever pitch of passion, the horror of remorse,
And the unbearable humiliation of being coldly rejected,
Were just a tiny foretaste of the torture I'm enduring
    now.
They love each other! How did they deceive me?
How did they get to see each other? When did it start?
Where?
You knew and you let me deceive myself!
Why didn't you tell me about their furtive affair?
Were they often seen talking together, seeking each
    other out?
Did they hide deep in the forest?
Oh! Nothing stood in their way.
Heaven looked on and smiled as they panted.

They went wherever desire took them, shamelessly.
Every day dawned, for them, serene and clear.
Whereas I, miserable abortion abhorred by all nature,
I hid from the day, I fled the light:
Death was the only God I dared address.
I waited for my life to end,
And fed on bile, and only drank my tears.
Even in my misery too closely observed,
I couldn't drown myself in my sorrows, as I'd have liked;
I savoured, shivering, that morbid pleasure;
And hiding my panic behind a calm façade,
Often I even had to go without tears.

ŒNON

There's no future in their love.
They won't see each other again.

PHEDRA

                    They will always love one another.
Even as I speak, ah! Perish the thought!
They're laughing at this madwoman.
Despite his exile which will separate them,
They swear never to part.
No, I can't bear their happiness – it's poisoning me,
Œnon. Pity me in my jealous rage.
We must get rid of Aricia. We must remind my husband
How he hates her loathsome race.
He must not draw the line at some light sentence:
The sister has outdone her murderous brothers.
I'll implore him in my jealous frenzy.
What am I doing? Am I out of my mind?
Me, jealous! Implore Theseus of all people!
My husband's alive, and my heart's still burning!

And who for? Who do I yearn for?
My every word makes my hair stand on end.
I've sunk as low as I can go.
I am incest and deceit incarnate now.
I want my hands dripping with innocent blood!
Monster! Yet I go on living; can still stare back at
The sacred sun from whom I am descended!
I am descended from the ruler of the Gods;
The heavens, the whole universe is filled with my
    ancestors.
Where can I hide? I could slip down into hell's dark
    night.
No I can't! My father's the keeper of the urn of the
    dead there;
Fate, they say, placed it in his stern hands:
Minos judges the quivering dead in hell.
Ah! Won't his appalled ghost shiver
When his daughter presents herself before him,
Forced to confess so many different sins,
And crimes perhaps unheard of even in hell!
What will you say, father, confronted by that horrible
    sight?
I believe I see you drop the dreaded urn;
I see you try to dream up some new punishment,
And turn into your own daughter's tormentor.
Forgive me. A cruel Goddess has ruined your family;
Can't you see, your sex-crazed daughter's her revenge!
Oh, but my poor body's never even fed
On that forbidden fruit I'm dying of desire for.
Catastrophe has pursued me to the bitter end;
In dying, I give up nothing but pain and turmoil.

ŒNON

    Madam, your fears are unfounded.

    To the outsider, it's just a lapse – and understandable.

    You're in love. No-one can fight their destiny.

    You were drawn in by a fatal spell.

    Is that so unheard of amongst human beings?

    Are you the only one love has triumphed over?

    'To err is human':

    You're human, accept human fate.

    You complain of being bound long ago in chains.

    Even the Gods, the Gods on high,

    Who send down thunderbolts to make the wicked quake,

    Have sometimes burned with illicit passion.

PHEDRA

    What, am I hearing right? Do you dare offer me more advice?

    You'd poison my mind till the very end, then,

    You witch! Look how you've destroyed me.

    The day I took flight, you dragged me back.

    Your pleading made me forget my duty.

    I was avoiding Hippolytus, and you made me see him.

    What did you think you were doing? How could your foul mouth

    Accuse him, and blacken his life?

    Perhaps he'll die because of it; perhaps his father's wild,

    Unholy wish has already been granted.

    I won't listen to you any more.

    Get out, you harpie,

    Go! Leave me to my doom.

    And may the just Gods give you your just deserts!

    May your punishment deter forever

All those who, like you, by foul means,
Prey on the weaknesses of unhappy rulers,
Telling them what they want to hear
And smoothing the way for their crimes;
Vile flatterers, the most deadly gift
Divine wrath could offer any ruler!

ŒNON, *alone*

Oh God! I did everything for her, left everything;
And this is what I get. I've earned it.

ACT V

Scene i – HIPPOLYTUS, ARICIA

ARICIA
    You're in mortal danger! How can you keep quiet
    And leave a father who loves you with the wrong idea?
    If you're so cruel my tears fail to move you,
    And you'll have no trouble not seeing me again,
    You'd better go, leave me here in misery;
    But you could at least save your life.
    Defend your honour against such slander,
    And make your father take back his wish.
    It's not too late. What stubborn whim
    Makes you leave the field open to your accuser?
    Tell Theseus everything.

HIPPOLYTUS
                  Ha! What haven't I told him?
    Should I have said how his bed's been polluted?
    Should I have told him what happened in gory detail,
    And make him blush for shame?
    You're the only one who guessed the truth.
    I can only pour my heart out to you and to the Gods.
    I couldn't hide from you what I wanted to hide from
       myself,
    That's how much I love you.
    But remember you are sworn to secrecy.
    Forget, if you can, what I've told you.

Don't ever part those innocent lips
To tell the horrible tale.
We'll leave it to the Gods:
It's in their interests to prove my innocence.
Sooner or later Phedra will be punished for her crime;
She'll get what she deserves.
There's only one thing I ask of you.
I can take care of the rest.
Shake off the slavery you've been reduced to;
Dare to follow, dare to come with me;
Break away from this deadly, desecrated place,
Where virtue chokes on poisoned air.
To cover your departure, profit by
The chaos my disgrace has caused.
I can guarantee your means of escape -
Until now no guards but mine have been assigned
     to you.
Powerful supporters will take up our defence;
Argos reaches out to us, and Sparta calls:
We'll share our grievances with our allies.
We can't let Phedra exploit our mutual disgrace,
And chase us both from my father's throne,
Promising her son both my estate and yours.
Now is our chance, we must take it.
You seem to hesitate? What's holding you back?
If I weren't thinking of your interests, I'd lack the
     courage.
Why, when I'm on fire, are you like ice?
Are you afraid of following in an exile's footsteps?

ARICIA
Oh, no! Exile would be bliss, my Lord!

If I could share your destiny, how happily
I'd live forgotten by the human race!
But since we're not united by so heavenly a bond,
How can I run away with you and maintain my honour?
I know that, without offending the strictest code of
   honour,
I can free myself from your father's chains:
After all, one is allowed to give tyrants the slip.
It's hardly like running away from home.
But you love me, my Lord, and my reputation
   warrants . . .

HIPPOLYTUS

No, no, I have too high a regard for your reputation.
I came to you with a more honourable plan:
Give your enemies the slip in your husband's arms;
We may suffer but at least we'd be free.
Exchanging vows depends on us alone.
We don't need wedding torches to be married;
At the gates of Troezen, among the graves,
The old burial grounds of the princes of my line,
There's a sacred temple feared by the faithless.
There, no mortal swears false oaths and lives.
The betrayer meets instant doom;
Fearing certain death there,
Liars curb their tongues.
That's where, if you believe in me, we'll pledge eternal
   love;
We'll take as witness the God who's worshipped there,
And beg him to serve as father.
I'll call on the most sacred Gods,
Chaste Diana, august Juno;

Each and every God, witnessing my love,
Will vouch for the sincerity of my holy vows.

ARICIA
The King is coming. Run, Prince, run.
I'll linger a moment to hide my departure.
Go. Leave me some guide I can trust
Who'll lead my trembling steps to you.

Scene ii – THESEUS, ARICIA, ISMEN

THESEUS
Oh Gods! Enlighten me, open my eyes to
The truth I'm searching for here.

ARICIA
Don't forget anything, Ismen, be ready to fly.

Scene iii – THESEUS, ARICIA

THESEUS
You've changed colour, you seem struck dumb.
What was Hippolytus doing here?

ARICIA
My Lord, he was saying goodbye forever.

THESEUS

> You won him with your eyes,
> His first amorous sighs were your doing.

ARICIA

> My Lord, it's true. I can't deny it:
> He hasn't inherited your unjust hate;
> He didn't treat me like a criminal.

THESEUS

> I understand: he swore eternal love.
> Don't be so stupidly taken in;
> He's promised others what he promised you.

ARICIA

> Hippolytus, my Lord?

THESEUS

> You ought to have made him less fickle.
> How could you bear to share him so horribly?

ARICIA

> And how can you allow such horrible calumny
> To mar the course of that untarnished life?
> How can you know him so little?
> Can't you tell the difference between guilt and innocence?
> Must a poisonous cloud conceal
> His dazzling virtue from your eyes alone?
> How could you sacrifice him like this to treacherous
>   tongues?
> Stop now: take back your murderous wish;
> Hope, my Lord, hope hard the cruel Gods
> Don't hate you enough to grant your wish.
> Often in their fury, they accept our sacrificial victims;

'When the Gods wish to punish us, they answer our
   prayers.'

THESEUS

It's useless, don't try and cover up for him.
Your love blinds you.
I believe loyal, irreproachable witnesses:
I've seen . . . I've seen real tears flow.

ARICIA

Take care, my Lord. With your invincible hands
You've rid us of countless monsters;
But you didn't get rid of them all; you spared
One . . .
Your son, my Lord, forbids me to go any further.
Knowing the respect he feels is still your due,
I'd hurt him too much if I dared go on.
I'll do as he does and keep quiet, and flee from you
So I can't be forced to break my silence.

Scene iv – THESEUS, *alone*

What can she mean? What's behind these words,
Begun so many times, and broken off?
Are they trying to trick me?
Plotting together to torture me?
And as for me: despite this severity,
What mournful voice cries out from the depths of
   my heart?

Pity pierces me to the marrow.
I must question Œnon a second time.
I must know more about this crime.
Guards, bring Œnon here to me, alone.

Scene v – THESEUS, PANOPE

PANOPE

I don't know what the Queen's contemplating,
My Lord, but I fear the worst:
She's death-white with despair.
Œnon was sent packing in shame,
And has thrown herself into the deep, dark sea.
We don't know what drove her to such an act of
    violence;
The waves have swept her away from us forever.

THESEUS

Why this?

PANOPE

            Her death hasn't stopped the Queen.
Anguish runs riot in her unsteady soul.
Sometimes, to soothe her secret sorrow,
She grabs her children and washes them with tears;
Then, suddenly rejecting maternal love,
She shoves them away from her in horror.
She wanders around in a daze.
Her eyes are wild, she doesn't know who we are.

Three times she's sat down to write and each time
She changes her mind and tears the letter up.
Please see her, my Lord, please help her.

THESEUS

Oh God! Œnon's dead and Phedra wants to die?
Bring my son back, let him defend himself!
Let him talk, I'll listen.
Neptune, don't fulfil your promise too soon.
I wish you'd never heard my prayer.
I might have been too ready to believe false witnesses
And raised my cruel hands to you too soon.
Ah! My despair will be endless, if my wish comes true!

Scene vi – THESEUS, THERAMENES

THESEUS

Theramenes, is that you? What have you done with
    my son?
I entrusted him to your care from the time he could
    crawl.
Why are there tears streaming down your face?
Where is my son?

THERAMENES

Your concern is touching, but it comes too late.
Your tenderness is wasted now! Hippolytus is gone.

THESEUS
No!

THERAMENES
My Lord, I watched him die:
The most wonderful of men, the most innocent.

THESEUS
My son's gone? It's not posssible: when I open my
arms to him,
The ruthless Gods speed up his death?
What sudden blow took him, what thunderbolt?

THERAMENES
We were just passing the gates of Troezen,
He was driving his chariot; his guards
Were grieving round him and shared his silence.
He followed the Mycenae road, lost in thought,
Letting his horses' reins float loosely.
Those superb stallions, that once so valiantly
Responded to the sound of his voice,
Now hung their heads and stumbled along
In forlorn sympathy.
Then a terrible cry, from far beneath the waves,
Rent the air;
And from the bowels of the earth a terrible voice
Groaned in answer.
Our blood froze in our veins.
The horses heard it, their manes stood on end.
Then, from the great flat sea,
Up bubbles a mountain of water:
The wave rolls in, breaks, and before our eyes,
Amongst the swirling foam, vomits a raging monster.

His huge head is armed with vicious horns;
His body all covered in sickly yellow scales;
Half raging bull, half dragon,
His rump's all wrinkled with writhing folds.
His great roars make the whole coast shake.
Heaven quakes, the earth trembles,
The air turns thick;
Even the wave that rolled him in shrinks back appalled.
Naturally everyone takes to their heels and
Hides in the temple nearby.
Hippolytus alone, son of his hero-father,
Reins in his steeds, grabs his spears and
Hurls himself at the monster, and with a deft hand,
Opens a big gash in the monster's side.
Writhing with rage and pain, the monster
Lurches forward and falls, howling, at the horses' feet;
It rolls over and turns its great flaming maw on them,
Covering them in a pall of fire and blood and smoke.
Terror finally gets the better of them; this time
    they're deaf,
They no longer hear Hippolytus' command or feel
    the bit.
His voice goes hoarse, his hands are torn,
The bit goes red with bloody foam.
They say, in the tumult, they even saw
A God stabbing the horses' sweaty haunches.
Fear drives them headlong over the rocks;
The axle screams and snaps in two. Fearless Hippolytus
Sees his chariot fly past him, smashed to pieces.
He himself gets caught up in the reins.
Forgive my grief. As long as I live,

I'll never get over what I saw.
I saw, my Lord, I saw your ill-fated son
Dragged by the horses his own hand had fed.
He tries to call them back, but his voice only frightens
    them
And they tear away. Soon his whole body is one big
    streak of blood.
The plain reverberates with our howls of pain.
Finally their frantic pace slackens:
They pull up, not far from the ancient tombs
Where his ancestors' cold bones lie.
We make for there, sobbing, his guards and I.
A thick trail of his abundant blood leads us to him:
Blood stains the rocks; clumps of his blood-matted hair
Are snagged on the thorny brambles.
I reach him, I call his name: he gives me his hand,
Opens a darkening eye, and shuts it a second later.
'Heaven', he says, 'snatches my innocent life from me.
Take care of poor Aricia when I'm gone.
Dear friend, if one day my father learns the truth,
And laments the fate of his wrongly-accused son,
To appease my blood and my wailing ghost,
Tell him to treat his captive gently;
He must give back to her . . . ' On that note our
    hero dies,
Leaving in my arms nothing but a broken shell,
A sad thing, tribute to the triumph of the wrathful
    Gods.
His own father wouldn't recognise him now.

THESEUS
    Oh my son! My dearest hope – I tore you from me!

Inexorable Gods, you served me only too well!
I'll go to my grave broken by regret.

THERAMENES
Then Aricia arrived.
She'd come, fleeing from you, my Lord,
To take him as her husband in the eyes of the Gods.
She comes closer: sees the red, smoking grass;
Sees – what a sight for a woman in love! -
Hippolytus stretched out, shapeless and pale.
At first she can't accept her loss;
Not recognising the hero she adores,
She sees Hippolytus yet keeps asking for him.
But in the end forced to admit he's lying in front of her,
With one mournful gaze she accuses the Gods,
Then cold, moaning, almost lifeless,
She falls unconscious at her beloved's feet.
Ismen is sobbing by her side and
Brings her back to life, back to grief.
Myself, I've come, cursing the sun that continues
    to shine,
To tell you his dying wishes: Your son. The hero.
So I perform, my Lord, the sad task
He entrusted to me with his dying breath.
But I see his mortal enemy is here.

Scene vii

THESEUS, PHEDRA, THERAMENES, PANOPE,
GUARDS

THESEUS

So! You've won: my son's life is over.
No wonder I'm afraid! No wonder a cruel suspicion
Gnaws at me and pardons him, in my heart of hearts!
Yes, Madam, he's dead, you may claim your victim:
Enjoy his destruction, just or unjust.
I prefer to let the truth stay hidden.
I believe him guilty, since you accuse him.
His death gives me reason enough to weep
Without my seeking some horrendous explanation,
Which will never bring him back to me,
But only intensify the pain.
Far away from you and from these shores,
Let me flee the bloody image of my mangled son.
Haunted by this memory,
I'd retreat from the whole world if I could.
Everything points at me;
My fame only adds to my torture:
If I were less well-known, it'd be easier to disappear.
I hate the Gods – down to the very gifts they've
    lavished upon me;
I'll live my life paying for their murderous favours;
I won't bore them any more with my futile prayers.
Whatever they've done for me, their deadly kindness
Can never make up for what they've taken from me.

PHEDRA

No, Theseus, I must break this unjust silence:

I must give your son back his innocence.
He was not guilty.

THESEUS

                    Oh! Cursed father that I am!
I condemned him on your word!
I suppose you think you've said enough . . .

PHEDRA

Every moment counts: Listen to me, Theseus.
I'm the one who looked upon your chaste and
    respectful son
With a lascivious, incestuous eye.
Venus set my soul on fire with lust;
That hateful Œnon took care of the rest.
She was worried Hippolytus, who knew of my
    obsession
And loathed me for it, would tell all.
The witch took advantage of my weakness,
And rushed to denounce him to you instead.
She's punished herself for it; I was outraged,
She fled and found an easy death beneath the sea.
I would have ended my life already with the sword,
But I couldn't leave tainted virtue unredeemed.
I wanted to die more slowly, showing you,
As I died, my remorse.
I have taken, I have poured into my burning veins,
A poison Medea brought with her from Crete.
It has already reached my heart,
Chilling the blood as my heart grows weak.
Already my vision's blurred and I can hardly see
The world or the husband I've so badly wronged.
Death steals the light from my eyes

And returns it to the day I darkened
With all its shining purity
Restored.

PANOPE

    She's dead, my Lord!

THESEUS

                 If only the memory
Of such an evil act could die with her!
Now that I see all too clearly,
Let us mix our tears with the blood of my unhappy son.
Let us go and embrace his remains,
And expiate the fury of a demented curse.
Let us honour him as he so well deserved;
And to appease his angry ghost,
Despite what her family have done,
I hereby claim his beloved as my daughter.